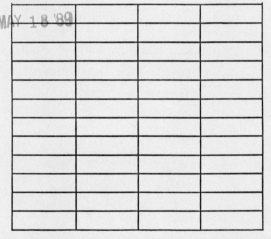

The Kingdom of the Franks

LIBRARY OF MEDIEVAL CIVILIZATION
EDITED BY
PROFESSOR DAVID TALBOT RICE

PETER LASKO

The Kingdom of
the Franks

NORTH-WEST EUROPE BEFORE
CHARLEMAGNE

McGRAW-HILL BOOK COMPANY · NEW YORK

Contents

Preface

This book originally constituted one chapter of a large volume which bore the title, *The Dark Ages*. There an attempt was made to give a brief account of the various civilizations and cultures that contributed to the building up of the arts and history of Europe when it first emerged as an independent entity round about the year 1000. The term 'Dark Ages' offered a useful portmanteau word to define the period from the temporal point of view; it comprised the phase from the decline of Roman power in the fourth century at least till the crowning of Charlemagne as Emperor of the West in the year 800, and at most till the turn of the millennium and the dawn of the Middle Ages properly speaking. But to describe as 'dark' the achievements and products of this age as a whole was very far from correct, for the age was by no means universally retrogressive. At the outset there flourished from 324 till 652 in Western Asia a civilization of great distinction under the rule of the Sassanian kings, which produced an art wherein a mass of very distinctive decorative motifs were developed, and they re-appeared again and again for many hundreds of years in the arts of almost every country from China to Britain. The importance of Sassanian art in the history of design can hardly be exaggerated. Further towards the West, in Armenia, a state was established where Christianity was adopted as the official religion even before it was recognized by Constantine in Italy, while a progressive architectural style was developed at least as early as the seventh century; in the tenth and eleventh centuries it was to be responsible for a series of remarkable innovations which were to be paralleled in the West a century or so later. Along the eastern fringes of the Mediterranean a progressive

Christian art flourished till it was eclipsed by Islam around 640; it exercised an influence even as far west as Ireland. Thereafter, under Muslim patronage, cultural ideas and themes in art were elaborated in the same area throughout the eighth, ninth and tenth centuries which were soon to affect western Europe very actively, both through trading contacts and as a result of the Crusades. On the eastern fringe of the European continent an even more important power was in being, that of Byzantium, where civilization reached peaks of brilliance which were to remain unsurpassed till the Renaissance, first around the middle of the sixth century, and again at the end of the ninth or early in the tenth. The first was characterized by a brilliantly original organic architectural system, the second by a supreme degree of craftsmanship and excellence in the minor arts, and both by a highly sophisticated pictorial style in painting and mosaic. If the other regions exercised an influence on the West so to speak behind the scenes, Byzantium was also overtly revered as a centre of inspiration in thought, culture and art not only throughout the whole Mediterranean sphere, but also further afield, in East and West alike; it was the supreme model of excellence that the rest of the world attempted to emulate.

Western Europe was certainly a good deal less advanced than the East, in any case until the ninth or tenth century. Yet it was not quite as dark an age as has sometimes been supposed. The Vikings boasted a developed non-representational art and they established contacts on the one hand with America and on the other with China. In Britain a stage had been reached in the more sophisticated arts by the end of the seventh century which was far in advance of anything elsewhere in the West. On the Continent there flourished three independent, though related, cultures all of which were to leave important legacies behind them; they were those of the Ostrogoths and Lombards in northern Italy, of the Visigoths in Spain and of the Merovingians and Franks in northern France and Germany. None of these can, perhaps, lay claim to be classed as civilizations, but in thought none of them was wholly backward looking, and each was responsible for the production of works of art of considerable historical significance and truly high aesthetic quality. Each left a legacy which exercised an important influence on developments which subsequently took place in Western Europe when once static urban regimes, like the Ottonian, had been established.

Our knowledge of the arts of these continental cultures, and to a certain degree that of their history also, is to a great extent based on the study of objects found in graves. It might be argued that the custom of burying valuable works of art with the corpse was essentially a barbarian practice, but it was a habit that died hard. Still, in the eighth and following centuries we find rich textiles and even pieces of jewellery being inserted into the tombs of noble or holy persons, like Charlemagne or St Cuthbert. It can thus hardly be counted as a slight against the Franks that the habit was, in their day, a universal one. It is in any case something for which we today must be extremely grateful, for it is largely thanks to this custom that we know as much as we do about the people and their arts, while a study of the decorative motifs on their arms and their jewellery tells us a good deal about their trading contacts and the political relationships that affected the Frankish state. And if at first the grave finds represent but one side of the culture, their evidence was, as time went on, supplemented by that offered by more sophisticated works, notably manuscript illuminations. This art was quite highly developed, and was in due course to influence very considerably the more advanced schools of manuscript illustration that were developed at the court and in a number of monasteries in the Carolingian age. True, the Merovingians were never responsible for the production of the more truly civilized arts such as major sculpture or wall painting; in the former respect northern Britain was well in advance of the Continent in the seventh century, and there is some evidence to suggest that wall paintings were also done there at that time. It was, however, not really till the establishment of the Carolingian empire at the end of the eighth century that really fine work in this vein was produced, and it might be said that only at that time did true civilization appear in Western Europe. Here the West was far behind Byzantium, even if its non-representational or its highly stylized animal arts did reach a very advanced stage. Many of the objects that Professor Lasko illustrates are not only very accomplished in this way, but are also truly beautiful.

Two of the chapters in the large volume on the Dark Ages have already been published in extended form, as separate books, one on the Vikings and one on Britain in Celtic and Saxon times. Both are closely concerned with Britain, for the role that the Vikings exercised on this country, especially in the north, was very considerable. The Frankish culture which Professor Lasko discusses in the pages that follow, was, on the other hand, wholly continental. But without some knowledge of what was happening in Europe it is impossible to gain anything like a complete picture even of cultural developments in Britain. The age with which he deals was a formative one; the art that was produced was, in its way, very significant, and had it not existed the subsequent story of culture in Europe would have been very different. Furthermore, it is an age about which we are still rather ignorant. So complete a selection of illustrations is nowhere else so readily accessible, nor is there to be found elsewhere so serviceable a general account. This volume should thus prove to be very essential reading for all who are interested in the making of Europe.

DAVID TALBOT RICE

Introduction

The centuries between the decline of the Roman empire in the west and the creation of a new western European empire by Charlemagne in the late eighth century have long been called the 'Dark Ages'. The term suggests a state of barbarism, a decay of civilized Mediterranean standards in the arts, in literature, in law and in stable government. And yet, during the Dark Ages, in the lands east and west of the Rhine, the foundations were laid on which Charlemagne was able to build.

Nor were the standards of material culture all that low. In textiles, pottery and glass, and even in the few fragments of architecture and architectural sculpture that have survived the zeal of later builders, we often find work of high quality, and in the products of the goldsmiths and metalworkers standards were reached which are unsurpassed in any other period of history.

Even in the literature of the period, in spite of what might be, and has been, called shortcomings of elegant grammar or style, the direct and vivid narratives of such historians as Gregory of Tours or the Venerable Bede are still able to excite our admiration today.

In fact, the use of the term 'Dark Ages' should be restricted to its basic meaning: to describe a period in which the sources of history are often dark indeed. What light it has been possible to shed on it is the result of bringing to bear on its problems all the disciplines of the modern historian – an intensive study, both textual and interpretative, of the scanty literary remains, the study of archaeology, art-history, numismatics and the study of place-names and linguistics.

To do full justice to the 'Dark Ages' in the Merovingian kingdom, is certainly a difficult, if not impossible, task. What is attempted here is merely to present some of the material splendour of the age, and to try to show that the decline of the standards of Mediterranean civilization did not create a vacuum in western Europe, but a challenge – indeed, the kind of challenge which does not basically differ from the challenge every generation of artists has to face. There would seem to be, on the face of it, no reason to suppose that the so-called 'Dark Ages' should have been less able than any other period of man's history to produce creative men; men who could apply themselves to the task of solving the new problems set by changing economic and social and political circumstances. It would be futile to consider whether the goldsmiths of the sixth and seventh centuries created work which is more or less 'great' than the Pantheon or Trajan's Column in Rome – the problems they solved differed completely from those of Roman architects, engineers or sculptors. It is how they solved their problems, with what creative ingenuity they set about their task, that gives us an insight into their civilization.

P.L.

Chapter One

The Rise of the Franks

Of all the barbarian peoples of the continent of Europe who infiltrated into and attacked the Roman empire of the west during the migration period, only the Franks succeeded in establishing a political power that survived the final disintegration of the empire, and eventually supplanted it. No one who lived at that time and who had witnessed the stirring events of the fourth or fifth centuries could have foreseen that the insignificant tribes of warriors, the Ripuarian and Salian Franks, were destined to lay the foundations of the culture which was to lead to the creation of the Carolingian empire, and, through it, to western European civilization as we *1* know it.

The Vandals had crossed the middle Rhine in 406, by 409 had reached Spain and by 439 established themselves as a commanding power in North Africa, with their headquarters in the ancient centre of the North African granaries of the Roman empire at Carthage. The Visigoths, probably some 10,000 in number, undertook a gigantic march from the lower Danube area, through the Balkans, then to Italy where their king, Alaric, took Rome itself in the year 410. They retreated to southern Gaul, settling there and in Spain, while the Ostrogoths, following upon their heels, settled in northern Italy, establishing a powerful kingdom under their great leader Theodoric, who was welcomed in Rome by the Pope, the senate and the people in AD 500. He was buried in his magnificent stone-built tomb just outside Ravenna in 526.

Settlers within Rome's frontiers

Compared with such dramatic events, the incursion of Frankish tribes across the Rhine from the mid-third century onwards must have seemed of no great importance. Their settlement as individual farmer/soldiers acting as defenders of the Roman frontier and known as *laeti*, probably began as early as the second century; indeed, such foreign settlers are already mentioned by the historian Tacitus (55–*c*.117). Larger tribal units, with similar military obligations – *foederati* or allied troops – began to be settled in the frontier by the mid-third century and during the following century such units, growing in size and importance, spread into more western areas of Roman Gaul. Basically it was such infiltration, rather than more direct conquests, which lay behind the growing Frankish power in Gaul.

We occasionally gain some strange sidelights on what must seem to us a cataclysmic series of events, leading to what is known as the 'collapse of the Roman empire'. History tells us of one Paulinus of Pella, a Gallo-Roman nobleman, who had Visigoths take over his estates near Bordeaux. Dispossessed, he became a 'refugee' – a status well known in our own times – and settled in straitened circumstances in Marseilles. From his correspondence we learn that a Goth, who wished to buy a certain small property that had once been his, actually sent him the price of it. Paulinus continues by complaining that the payment does not represent anything like its true value, but declares himself grateful for such an unexpected windfall to aid his attempts to build a new life for himself. There could be no better evidence of an astonishing continuity of law in a period so often seen as one of traumatic change and collapse. If this was true of the war-like trek of the Visigoths into southern Gaul, how much truer must such acceptance of Roman standards have been among the Franks, who had been absorbed into Roman Gaul over such a long period of time.

Who were the Franks and where did they originate? The available evidence seems sufficient only to suggest that they were a political amalgamation of many small tribes which took place in the first and second centuries A D in the lands between the river Weser and the Rhine. The names of Germanic

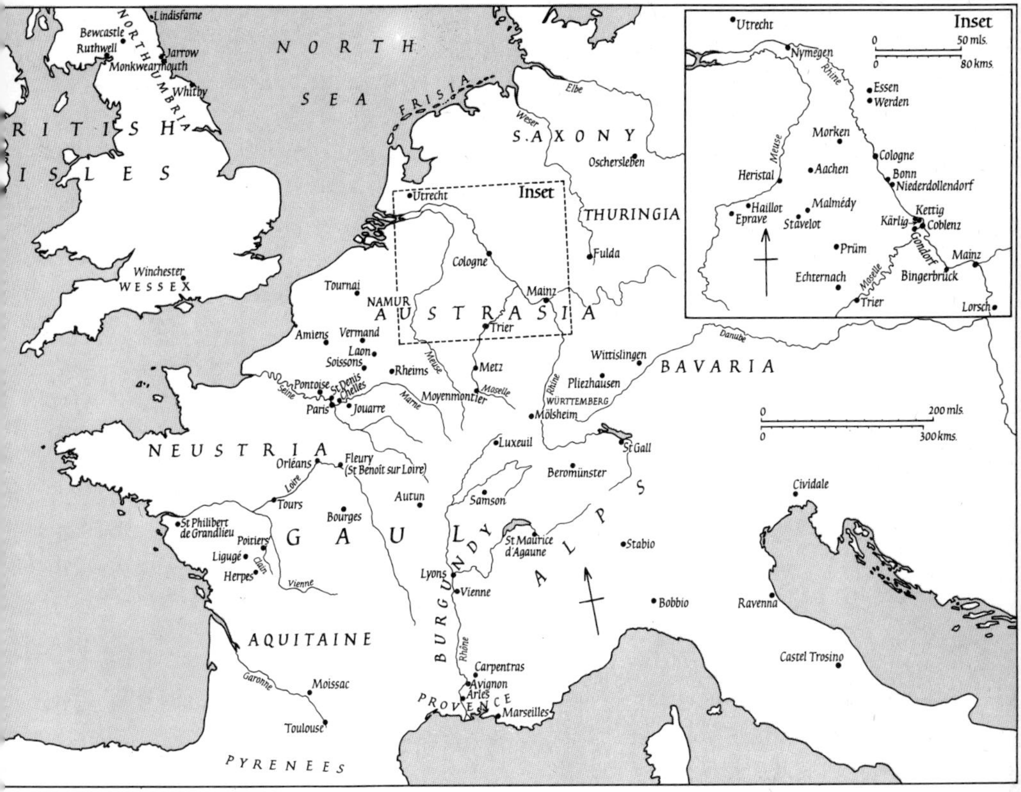
NORTH SEA
BRITISH ISLES
NORTHUMBRIA
Lindisfarne
Bewcastle
Ruthwell
Jarrow
Monkwearmouth
Whitby
WESSEX
Winchester
FRISIA
SAXONY
Oschersleben
THURINGIA
Fulda
Elbe
Weser
Utrecht
Inset
Cologne
Mainz
Trier
Tournai
NAMUR
AUSTRASIA
Amiens
Vermand
Laon
Soissons
Rheims
Metz
Pontoise
St Denis
Chelles
Paris
Jouarre
Seine
Marne
Meuse
Moselle
Moyenmontier
Rhine
WÜRTTEMBERG
Mölsheim
Wittislingen
Pliezhausen
BAVARIA
Danube
Luxeuil
St Gall
Beromünster
NEUSTRIA
Orléans
Loire
Fleury
(St Benoît sur Loire)
Autun
Samson
Tours
Bourges
St Philibert
de Grandlieu
Poitiers
Ligugé
Herpes
Clain
Vienne
GAUL
BURGUNDY
St Maurice
d'Agaune
Stabio
ALPS
Lyons
Vienne
Bobbio
Ravenna
Cividale
Castel Trosino
AQUITAINE
Rhône
Carpentras
Avignon
Arles
PROVENCE
Marseilles
Garonne
Moissac
Toulouse
PYRENEES
0 200 mls.
0 300 kms.
Inset
0 50 mls.
0 80 kms.
Utrecht
Nymegen
Rhine
Essen
Werden
Morken
Meuse
Cologne
Heristal
Aachen
Bonn
Niederdollendorf
Haillot
Eprave
Malmédy
Stavelot
Kettig
Kärlig
Coblenz
Gondorf
Prüm
Mainz
Echternach
Moselle
Bingerbrück
Trier
Lorsch

1 Europe between the fifth and eight centuries. Sites shown are major find spots and ecclesiastical centres mentioned in the text. The Franks rapidly increased their settlement west of the Rhine early in the fifth century. Other more powerful barbarian peoples surrounded them, and they were neither united nor particularly numerous, yet in about fifty years (464–511), they had succeeded in defeating or conciliating all their rivals and becoming one of the supreme powers of post-Roman Europe

tribes such as Franks, Alamanni, Thuringians and so on, indicate larger groups of peoples, which superseded the smaller, older and far more numerous tribal units who inhabited the forests east of the Rhine at the height of Roman imperial power. Just as little is known of their material culture before they came under the influence of Roman civilization as is known of their tribal origins.

It is only from the material excavated from the cemeteries of the *laeti* and *foederati* from the fourth century onwards, that any picture emerges of Germanic culture. These cemeteries are known as *Reihengräber*, or Row-grave cemeteries, a name given them because their graves are arrayed in more or less clearly defined rows, with the heads usually pointing towards the west. Such cemeteries are found in the frontier areas of the empire stretching from Britain, northern France and Belgium in the west, to the Danube and the Black Sea in the south and east. The men are buried with their weapons and the women with their jewellery, as was customary among the Germanic peoples, but the mere fact that these cemeteries contain inhumations (as against the cremation practised by their forefathers) shows the extent to which they were already under the influence of Roman custom. It is in the *Reihengräber* cemeteries, therefore, that we must look for the beginnings of Frankish art.

Earliest Frankish Art

The weapons, the buckles, and in fact most of the military equipment buried with the *laeti* and *foederati* show that their taste in decoration was little more than a somewhat provincial, and at times barbarized, version of Roman forms. The finest of these buckles and brooches mostly belong to the second half of the fourth century and are made in a technique which is called 'chip-carving'. This entails lines being gouged out of a flat surface with the cuts of a knife held at 45 degrees to it, resulting in a glittering array or triangular-sectioned channels. Cast in bronze which was often gilt, or occasionally, in pieces of finer quality, cast in silver, the technique was almost certainly developed from the *cire-perdue* (lost wax) method of casting, in which the original 'model' is cut out of wax, which lends itself extremely well to easy and rapid cuts of the knife. The wax 'model' is then encased in clay and fired in a kiln, which melts the wax out of the mould. The wax is then replaced by the molten metal.

2–4

2–4 Buckle *above*, decorative ring *below*, and spear-mount *right*, all in silver, niello inlay and partly gilt, from the late fourth-century cemetery at Vermand. The chip-carved designs are typically Roman, including a cicada at the top of the mount, relatively naturalistic animal ornament, rosettes and an interlaced star

17

The designs employed – palmettes, spirals, key patterns and animal terminals – are all clearly of Roman origin and they sometimes include, in the most sumptuous bronze examples, typically Roman portrait busts in inlaid silver. Poorer quality work often has a degree of abstraction and an emphasis on flattened and stylized animal forms. It is difficult to say whether this more 'abstract' art is the result of the more 'native' Germanic taste of the settlers, less closely linked with the mainstream of Roman culture, or whether it is merely due to less expert and less civilized workmanship practised among the lower social classes of the indigenous Gallo-Roman population. Perhaps it is just the result of the mass production of poor-quality military equipment. One thing is certain, that these simply decorated objects of daily use are found only in the area forming the frontier zones of the Roman empire. Also, there is little distinction in styles between the north – including even the southern areas of the British Isles – and the south right down to the lower reaches of the Danube. This must surely be evidence that the material is basically Roman, under little, if any, influence from Germanic settlers, because it is only the Roman element that is constant along the entire length of the imperial frontier.

5   Bronze buckle from Colchester, the bow made up of 'dolphins'. A typical
late Roman military buckle

6   Multi-coloured glass goblet, of so-called 'diatret' glass, found at Niederemmel,
near Trier. A superb product of the Late Roman glass industry in the Rhineland,
which is partly blown and partly cut, and includes a delicate outer 'net'-like
design

7　Early Frankish glass 'claw' beaker, found at Nettersheim. The Roman glass industry in the Rhineland continued without break into the Merovingian period, and created a tradition of high technical skill, and a developing repertoire of forms

The famous cemeteries at Vermand, Samson and Eprave, as well as the more recently excavated cemetery at Haillot in the Namur region, provide us with material from the vital period between the late fourth and the beginning of the sixth century, which saw the change of the Salian Franks from their status of *foederati*, settled mainly in the frontier region, through their expansion far deeper into Gaul and the defeat of the last Roman ruler in Gaul, Syagrius, in 486, to the foundation of an independent Frankish kingdom. After this, the social pattern of the country was set for several centuries. The population consisted of two separate elements – the conquering Franks and the conquered Gallo-Romans. They had different customs, and for a time lived under different laws, but, as we shall see, the essence of later Merovingian culture lies in their eventual fusion.

Much of the material in these cemeteries, especially the pottery and glass, is fundamentally Late Roman in every way. Certainly, the Roman glass industry in the cities of the 6–7 Rhineland and the lower Rhine region continued to flourish under the increasing control of the Franks – as did the pottery industry everywhere. Metalwork, however, and especially the weapons, show changes towards Frankish types, and in the latest graves of the early sixth century we begin to find examples of cloisonné jewellery that certainly could no longer be confused with Gallo-Roman work. But above all, it is in the animal art developed in this period out of Roman prototypes that we must seek the beginnings of Germanic art.

The analysis and dating of these decorative animal styles have perhaps been dominated far too long by the typological approach first firmly established by the pioneer archaeologist Bernard Salin in his *Die Altgermanische Thierornamentik*, published in Stockholm in 1904. Alongside the spirals, key-patterns and palmettes, clearly Roman in origin, we find simple, flat animal forms, either as complete quadrupeds, often crouching, or as head terminals. At first complete in form, but with clearly defined limbs, they become separated

8, 9 Details of two fifth-century gold collars, from Oland *above*, and Väster-gotland *below*. Both show fine filigree and granulation. In the example below, the rigid forms of Style I appear, while in the other more ribbon-like and fluid forms are used

10 Gold scabbard mount from Södermanland. Another example of the relatively early use of flowing rather than of rigidly segmented forms. For a discussion
of *Illus. 8–10, see also* pp. 58–61

into their constituent parts and are re-assembled into a
satisfying decorative whole, frequently distorted to fill the
most varied shapes on parts of brooches and buckles. This
animal art was first defined by Salin as 'Style I'. In a typological sense, it is seen to be derived out of the flaccid forms
of Late Roman dolphins and animal-head terminals, and was
developed by Germanic craftsmen of succeeding generations
(not only among the Franks, but even more successfully
among the Germanic peoples in their homeland, especially
in Scandinavia), into an incredibly rich, ever more varied   *8–10*
and imaginative style. It is doubtful, however, that such a
development should be seen in such a strictly typological and
chronological way. Abstraction of animal forms must not be
seen simply as a deterioration of naturalistic forms, mis-
understood by succeeding craftsmen. The seeds of such
abstraction can certainly be found in early work of high

23

quality, as well as in the poor-quality products of Roman military equipment. Indeed, it is probably true to say that the progress towards more and more abstract and bisected forms, spread in lavish profusion over the whole surface to be decorated, was more rapid in gold- and silverwork, by definition for aristocratic patrons, than in the poorer and more widespread bronze material.

11   Thus a synthesis was created of the abstract tastes of the new aristocracy and the sophisticated techniques of metalwork, glass manufacture and goldsmith's work of the later Roman empire.

Probably of even greater importance to the development of styles in western Europe at this time, was the movement of peoples from the east to the west – the Visigoths, the Ostrogoths and especially the invading Huns under Attila, defeated by the Romans, with the help of the Franks and other Germanic settlers, near Troyes in 451. They brought with them the tastes and techniques of the peoples beyond the eastern borders of the Roman empire, Iranians, Parthians and Avars, and the tastes also of those who lived within the eastern provinces of the empire itself.

11   Gold bracteate from Västergotland. Such decorative gold pendants are often based on Late Roman coin types. (*See also* pp. 58–61 and *Illus. 53.*) Here the rhythmic and linear body of the creature terminates in a bird-like head and beak at the top right

Chapter Two

Childeric and the Coming of Christianity

The Son of Merovech

The first compelling evidence of eastern influence can be found in the tomb of the earliest of the great Frankish rulers, Childeric, whose rich burial was accidentally discovered at *12–20* Tournai in 1653. The son of the half-legendary Merovech, from which the name of the Merovingian dynasty is derived, he died in 482. Only a few fragments of this find have survived, the bulk of it having been stolen when thieves broke into the Imperial Art Gallery in Paris in 1831. Fortunately all the finds had been published soon after their discovery by the Antwerp physician, Jean-Jacques Chifflet, who supplemented his careful descriptions with excellent illustrations. The grave was certainly that of Childeric, because it contained a gold signet ring engraved with a full-face portrait of the king and the legend: CHILDERICI REGIS – *13, 15* only a cast or two of this important seal ring now survive. In addition to this ring two swords were found in the tomb, *12, 14* both heavily ornamented with gold and cloisonné garnet inlay – they are among the earliest examples of polychrome jewellery so far found in a Frankish grave. Also in the grave were Childeric's typically Frankish battle-axe, his spear and the head of his horse with all its harness, numerous gold buckles, gold mounts from a belt, a heavy gold torc, a *17* mounted crystal ball, and a purse with a hundred gold coins as well as a treasure of two hundred silver coins. No less than *19, 20* three hundred gold cicadas, the symbol of eternal life, their wings inlaid with garnets, were sewn on the king's brocaded cloak. No Frankish burial of comparable wealth has ever

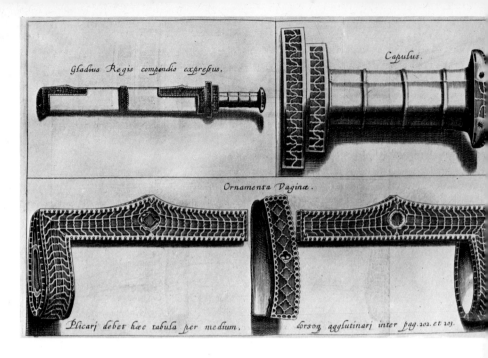

Gladius Regis compendio expressus.

Capulus.

Ornamenta Vaginae.

Plicari debet haec tabula per medium.

dorsoq agglutinari inter pag. 202. et 203.

been discovered since, and only the Sutton Hoo burial in East Anglia rivals its wealth in the entire Dark Ages.

Apart from the wealth of the tomb of Childeric, its archaeological importance can hardly be overestimated. It is firmly dated by the king's death, and its contents show us that the art of the court bore little, if any, relation to the mass of the material found in the *Reihengräber* cemeteries. The incipient animal art of the bronze buckles and brooches found little echo at the court, where the richer flavour of eastern art-forms played a predominant part. Indeed, in this tomb of a Germanic king near the northern borders of the empire we find a reflection of the orientalizing tastes that can be traced in upper layers of Late Roman society wherever it survived in the fifth century – in north Italy, in Rome itself and, of course, more especially at the court of Constantinople. In the art which he adopted Childeric shows that he saw himself as a successor to the Roman rulers of Gaul, ready to absorb their cultural aspirations. Clearly no Germanic animal style was yet worthy of a place at court.

12–14 Finds from the tomb of Childeric
(*d.* 482). The plate from Chifflet's publication of
1655 on the left, when compared to the few
surviving pieces opposite, is evidence of the
remarkable accuracy of the early engravings.
Left and right, the sword hilt and scabbard
mounts, with a plausible reconstruction. *Below,*
a modern replica of Childeric's seal ring, and an
impression from it. *See also Illus. 15*

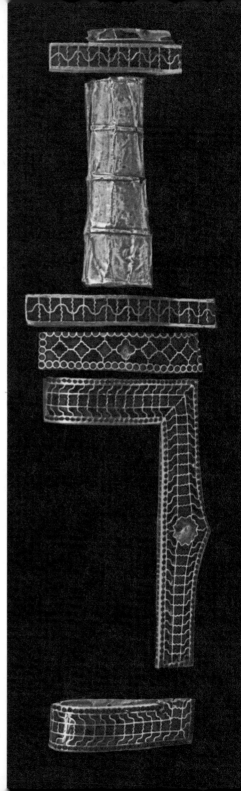

15 Group of rings from Chifflet's publication, showing in the centre Childeric's seal-ring stolen in 1831, now known only from casts made before that date. The sard above is antique, but the sapphire below, clearly late medieval, cannot be from the Childeric tomb

28

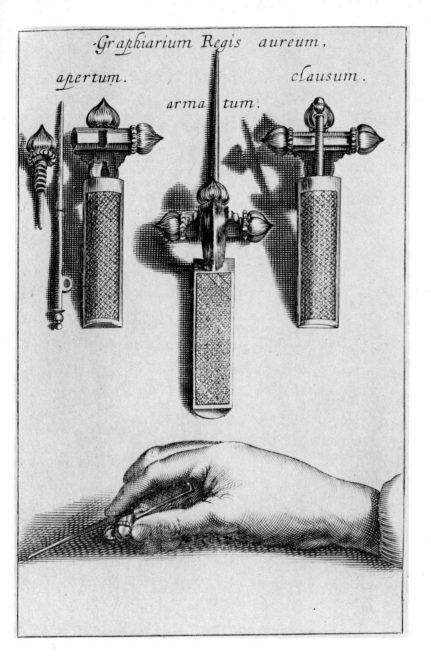

Graphiarium Regis aureum,

apertum.   *clausum.*

arma tum.

16   A typical and well-known Late Roman fibula found in Childeric's tomb. It is interesting to note that Chifflet has mis-interpreted this brooch as the King's gold stylus. Below he shows how he imagined it being used to write on wax tablets

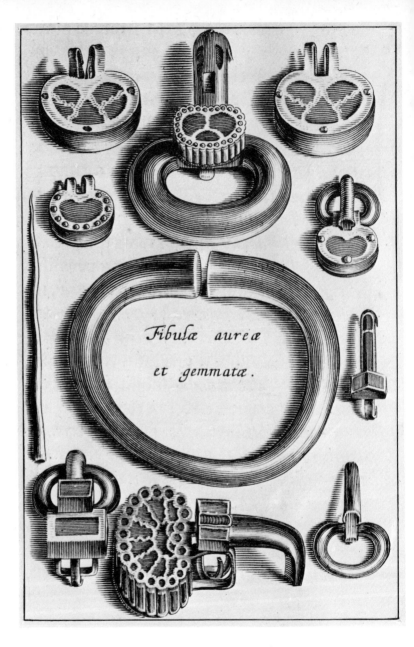

Fibulæ aureæ

et gemmatæ.

17　Gold buckles with garnet inlay in stepped cells and, in the centre, a gold torc bracelet; another page in Chifflet's publication of the finds in Childeric's tomb, discovered at Tournai in 1653

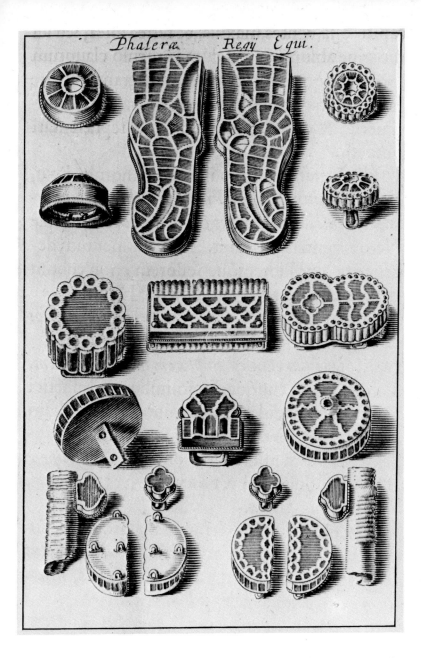

Phaleræ Regij Equi.

18 At the top, two strap-ends are examples of the rare use of Germanic animal ornament in this treasure. The small mounts, *top left*, are among the few pieces to have survived the robbery of 1831

31

19 Several hundred coins were found in Childeric's tomb. *Above*, three silver denarii of the second century AD, and a silver siliqua of the fourth century. *Left*, a silver tetradrachm of Iysamichos, showing the head of Alexander the Great. Chifflet described it as a bronze coin, which is not possible

20 Examples of the Byzantine gold solidi of the fourth and fifth centuries from the tomb, many of which have survived and are still in the collection of the Bibliothèque Nationale, Paris

Probably much the same attitude persisted at the court, during the period of rapid Frankish expansion, under the greatest of their rulers, Childeric's son Clovis, although this would be difficult to prove. It was Clovis who had finally put an end to Roman rule in northern Gaul by the defeat of Syagrius at Soissons in 486. In the same year Clovis, who was only twenty, having succeeded to the throne at the age of fifteen, mounted his first attack on the Thuringians – thus beginning the process of making himself ruler of all the Germans. In 496 he conquered the Alamanni and defeated the Visigoths at Tours. A few years earlier he had married Clotilda, niece of the king of Burgundy, who had been converted to the Catholic faith, and after the defeat of the Visigoths, probably in 503, Clovis himself was baptized an orthodox Catholic either at Tours or at Rheims.

Although born and brought up a pagan, Clovis seems always to have respected the Church. The story of the chalice of Soissons is evidence for this, as well as shedding light on the nature of his authority as king and on his own personal character. After the taking of Soissons a sacred chalice of the Christians was part of the loot seized by the army. Clovis tried to save it for the Church, but one of his soldiers objected that the king was not to have more than his fair share, and cut it in half with a stroke of his axe. Clovis had to submit to Frankish custom, but at the next opportunity clove the soldier's skull saying, we are told, 'Thus didst thou treat the chalice of Soissons.'

Clovis' conversion to Catholicism was of the greatest importance to the subsequent history of the Franks. By it he obtained for himself the goodwill and even the support of the Gallo-Roman population of Gaul against his powerful Germanic neighbours, the Visigoths, the Ostrogoths and the Burgundians – all of whom subscribed to the Arian heresy. This form of Christian belief held that there was only one Divinity – God. Catholicism, or 'orthodoxy' as it became known, taught the divinity of the Trinity: God the Father, God the Son and God the Holy Ghost. Arianism seems to have appealed to the Germanic peoples converted to Christianity – perhaps because they found it easier to accept Christ as a man than as a divine being. The support of the orthodox majority of the Gallo-Roman population gained by Clovis' conversion was symbolized by his being granted an honorary consulship by the eastern emperor Anastasius in 508. By his conversion, therefore, the position of Clovis was immeasurably strengthened and a firm base was created for Frankish rule in Gaul. Clovis had, by design or by the accident of his marriage to a Catholic princess, placed himself firmly on what was to be the winning side in the Arian controversy, a controversy which bedevilled the relationship of all the other Germanic rulers with the indigenous populations of the areas they attempted to control in spite of insufficient land settlement by their own people.

One more danger faced by the other Germanic peoples, who also stood in line of succession to the Roman empire, was their total absorption into Mediterranean life, cut off from their homelands. Clovis' strength lay in his geographical position, which forced him to create a new centre of power in the north-west of Europe and at the same time enabled him to remain in contact with the German homelands. Not that these homelands, now for the most part under the control of Saxon tribes, were friendly to Frankish rule – far from it – but it was there, in the sixth and seventh centuries, that a new northern culture was created which was to rival Roman humanism in importance as an ingredient of nascent western culture.

Classical Models

What evidence we have of the period of Clovis' reign suggests that his cultural aspirations did not differ much from those of his father. Only his acceptance of Christianity and, subsequently, his support of the Gallo-Roman Church and the support that he received from it add a new dimension to the period. Of the rare pieces of early church plate to survive, the Gourdon chalice and paten are likely to date from 21 his reign. They are ornamented with coloured inlay, now partially lost, and show clearly a synthesis of Roman forms and the orientalizing barbaric taste for rich and colourful decoration similar to that observed in Childeric's grave goods. The chalice is in the shape of a Roman decorative vase while the so-called paten, perhaps more probably a small portable altar, is decorated with the colourful stepped cell-work inlay which was to play such a large part in Germanic polychrome jewellery of the succeeding century.

21   Gold chalice and the so-called paten from Gourdon. The large cross in the centre of the 'paten' and the four smaller crosses in the corners of the inlaid border, might support the argument that it is a portable altar, these dedication crosses being usual on such altars

Architecture

Of the architecture of the period next to nothing survives above ground although we know that it must, of course, have existed. The Gallo-Roman Church had been growing in strength and power long before Clovis' conversion. Already in the second century the bishoprics of Lyons, Marseilles and Vienne had been founded, and in the third century eight more had been added in Gaul, from Toulouse in the south to Trier in the north, while in the fourth century the bishoprics of Cologne and Mainz had been created. Early in the fifth century monasteries, mostly as yet in the south, like the island off the Provençal coast – Lérins – and St Victor at Marseilles, were also founded.

Obviously much building activity was undertaken. We know, for example, of Bishop Nicetius' (526–66) rebuilding of the 'Double Cathedral' of Trier, which had suffered destruction a hundred years earlier. Gregory of Tours speaks of the building of many churches, some of these of considerable size. The basilica of St Martin at Tours, he tells us, was 160 ft long, 60 ft wide, and 45 ft high as far as the ceiling. The building had 32 windows in the sanctuary, 20 in the nave, and 41 columns. In the whole structure there were 120 columns and 8 doors, 3 in the sanctuary and 5 in the nave. Gregory proudly adds that the four rows of columns in St Peters in Rome numbered only 96 in all and therefore were fewer in number than those used in the church of St Martin at Tours. At Clermont, Bishop Namatius had built a cathedral church, a cruciform basilica, with a rounded apse and two aisles. It was 150 ft long, 60 ft wide, and 50 ft high from floor to ceiling, with 70 columns, 42 windows and 8 doors, while 'the walls of the sanctuary were lined with marble of different kinds'. His descriptions, unfortunately, give us very little idea of the actual form of these buildings. All we learn is that churches were of the basilican type with two aisles, often had rounded apses, sometimes had transepts, and that the interior ceilings were made of wood. Whether galleries above

22

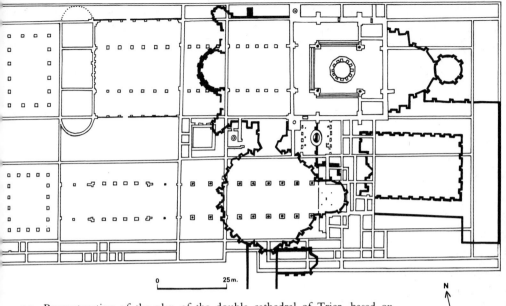

22 Reconstruction of the plan of the double cathedral of Trier, based on excavations, drawn over the outline of the present cathedral and the neighbouring church of Our Lady. The double cathedral, first laid out soon after 325, is here seen as it was about the year 400, after the east end of the northern church had a square 'martyrium' added c. 380. At the instigation of Bishop Nicetius the building was almost wholly restored, only the size of the atrium being reduced

aisles were built is difficult to discover, but it is hard to see how nearly 80 columns could have been used in the nave of the church at Tours, without a gallery. A nave of 160 ft in length could hardly have had more than 8 to 10 bays. If we count the arcade only, this gives only 19 to 20 columns and if the aisles had attached shafts, we might have another 20, making a total of 40. If the galleries above the aisles had triple openings carried on two columns each, another 32 columns would bring us very close to Gregory's total. Without galleries, we would need to think of double aisles (i.e. four rows of columns) like those of the great Roman basilicas of the fifth century, including St Peter's in Rome. Had this been the case, Gregory would almost certainly have made this comparison when he mentions the first church of Christendom in the same paragraph.

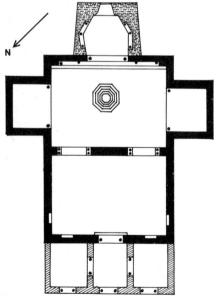

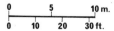

23, 24   The exterior of the baptistery of St Jean at Poitiers, seen from the south-east, with the plan below. The building, probably of fifth-century date, was considerably altered in the seventh century, making use of Roman brick

25 Detail of the south front of the baptistery of St Jean, Poitiers. One of the
very rare architectural survivals of the period

26 Interior of the St Jean baptistery. The larger, earlier, windows were blocked in and decoration added in the seventh century. The interior capitals are late antique and the abaci are early medieval insertions

Crypts were common and, it seems, vaulted. At St Venerandus at Clermont, Gregory reports that the vault had become ruinous and collapsed, and at Langres the bishop rebuilt the crypt in the sixth century, 'vaulting it in elegant style'. Where a transept was built, the crossing may have been covered by a tall lantern, almost certainly built of wood. At the west end a porch or narthex was usually found and, to the west of that, an atrium surrounded by arcades is mentioned a number of times by Gregory. Not only have the buildings themselves been destroyed but, with them, their rich interior decoration of wall-painting and mosaic. Gregory tells us that the wife of Bishop Namatius at Clermont 'sat with a book on her knees directing the painters' in the church of St Stephen outside the Walls which she had founded. The book was perhaps a painter's pattern book (again, none have survived) or perhaps more likely a richly illuminated manuscript from the cathedral library, which she used to give iconographical guidance to the painters.

The skill of Gaulish masons is attested, admittedly later on at the end of the seventh century, by Bede's reference to masons being imported into Northumbria from Gaul, because of their superior ability in cutting stone. Perhaps something of fifth-century architectural style survives in the baptistery of St Jean at Poitiers, in spite of many additions and *23–26* alterations made in the seventh century and later. Roman brick is the main building material employed here, and the cornices, pediments and other architectural details are un-compromisingly Roman in derivation. There is, of course, little reason to suppose that Frankish builders, skilled no doubt only in timber and half-timbered building, could add anything to Roman traditional methods and materials. Architectural carving, too, as can be seen in such rare survivals as the fifth-century capitals from 'La Daurade' at *27, 28* Toulouse, was entirely dependent on Roman traditions.

27, 28   Fifth-century marble capital and part of a carved shaft from the church of Notre-Dame de la Dourade

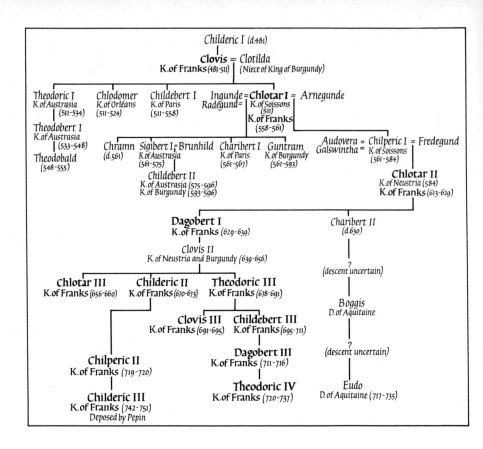

Childeric I (d.481)
|
Clovis = Clotilda
K.of Franks (481-511) | (Niece of King of Burgundy)

Theodoric I — K.of Austrasia (511-534)
Theodobert I — K.of Austrasia (533-548)
Theodobald (548-555)

Chlodomer — K.of Orléans (511-524)

Childebert I — K.of Paris (511-558)

Ingunde = **Chlotar I** = Arnegunde
Radegund = | K.of Soissons (511)
K.of Franks (558-561)

Chramn (d.561)

Sigibert I = Brunhild — K.of Austrasia (561-575)
Childebert II — K.of Austrasia (575-596) / K.of Burgundy (593-596)

Charibert I — K.of Paris (561-567)

Guntram — K.of Burgundy (561-593)

Audovera = **Chilperic I** = Fredegund
Galswintha = K.of Soissons (561-584)

Chlotar II — K.of Neustria (584) / K.of Franks (613-629)

Dagobert I — K.of Franks (629-639)
Clovis II — K.of Neustria and Burgundy (639-656)

Chlotar III — K.of Franks (656-660)
Childeric II — K.of Franks (670-673)
Theodoric III — K.of Franks (678-691)

Clovis III — K.of Franks (691-695)
Childebert III — K.of Franks (695-711)

Chilperic II — K.of Franks (719-720)
Childeric III — K.of Franks (742-751) Deposed by Pepin

Dagobert III — K.of Franks (711-716)
Theodoric IV — K.of Franks (720-737)

Charibert II (d.630)
?
(descent uncertain)

Boggis D.of Aquitaine
?
(descent uncertain)

Eudo D.of Aquitaine (717-735)

Frankish Power Grows

29 At the death of Clovis in 511, his kingdom was divided among his four sons according to Frankish custom. This had its obvious disadvantages, leading to the constant division of the kingdom. Clovis avoided the worst results of this by dividing each part of his kingdom, rather than the kingdom itself, into four parts, and each of his sons received a part of the homelands and each a part of the conquests Clovis had added to his realm. As a result none of the sons had a sufficiently unified territory to attempt sole rule, and Paris, the chief seat of the kingdom, was given into the control of all four sons. It was not the 'kingdom' but the 'royal domains' – the wealth of the king – that was divided equally among the sons. Yet,

42

29 Genealogical table of the Merovingian dynasty. The rulers of the entire kingdom are shown in heavy type

30, 31 Representative groups, up to the sixth century, of grave-goods other than weapons. *Right*, finds from the cemetery at Herpes (Charente) and, *below*, a selection of objects from northern France and Rhineland graves, including a glass drinking horn from Bingerbruck and a striped glass bowl from Rheims

32 Gold coin of Theodobert I (533–48), grandson of Clovis. The design of the coin is based on contemporary Byzantine gold solidi

even so, the arrangement did not avoid dissension within the family. The second son, Clodmir, died in 524 and the others murdered his children in order to divide his share among themselves. The eldest, Theodoric, died in 534 and his only surviving grandson in 555. The third, Childebert, died in 558, leaving the youngest, Chlotar I, in possession of the whole kingdom. His own son rebelled against him – 'like Absalom' says Gregory of Tours – but Chlotar defeated him, shut him up in a hut with his wife and family and burned them all to death, an action for which he later seems to have felt no little remorse.

Despite these troubles the Frankish kingdom continued to expand, and by AD 534 Burgundy came under Frankish rule, the Rhône valley and Marseilles were incorporated into the kingdom, the Bavarians were conquered, and even the Saxons east of the Rhine were beaten back and forced to pay tribute to the Frankish kings. Before the middle of the sixth century, the Frankish borders were extended as far east as the middle Danube. Frankish warriors under Clovis' grand-son Theodobert even crossed the Alps to take advantage of the struggle between the Ostrogoths and the Byzantine emperor Justinian. But with the death of Theodobert in 548 this ambitious campaign came to an end: the Merovingian kingdom had reached the point of its greatest expansion – not to be substantially surpassed until the time of Charlemagne.

In spite of the widespread adoption of the Christian faith, cemetery material still abounds in the sixth and seventh centuries. It supplies us with a vast quantity of weapons, brooches and buckles, ornaments, pins, pottery and glass,

32

30, 31

44

33   A pair of sixth-century gold S-shaped
brooches with animal head terminals, inlaid
with garnets, from Diesslingen

which serve to throw considerable light on the culture of the
time. The number of sites that have yielded material of this
kind is quite staggering – in Württemberg alone, for example,
an Alamannic area, nearly 800 different cemeteries have been
recorded, some containing more than 300 individual burials.
Altogether, something like 40,000 burials were estimated to
have been excavated in Europe by 1961. The ornamental
styles of the brooches, buckles, pins, etc., differ, of course, in
the different areas of the Frankish kingdom, but it is clear that
in the sixth century certain basic stylistic elements gained a
wide popularity over the greater part of the area. Such
elements are the 'chip-carved' techniques in the spiral, key
and fret patterns, inlaid garnets and filigree ornamentation,
radiated brooches with straight foot or with lozenge foot
terminating in animal heads. Bird forms, too, usually with
long curving heads, or fish-shaped ornaments are employed   *33, 34*
as the heads of pins or as small mounts or brooches in their
own right. A large and varied vocabulary of forms makes up
the vast quantity of finds from the Germanic cemeteries of the
period.

34   A pair of sixth-century gold brooches in
the form of fishes, inlaid with garnets, from
Bülach, near Zurich

Chapter Three

The Aristocratic Tombs at Cologne and St Denis

Until recent years only 'average' material dominated the study of Frankish archaeology, and nothing seemed to survive to bridge the gap between the royal riches of Childeric's tomb of 482 and the wealth of aristocratic creation connected with the court of Charlemagne some three hundred years later. Only occasionally, in graves of the minor aristocracy like the early seventh-century tomb of a warrior at Morken, excavated in 1955, or that at Wittislingen of the later seventh century, did splendid finds give some indication of the standard of workmanship and material wealth one might have expected to find among the richer sections of Merovingian society. The burials discovered recently under the cathedral of Cologne and the abbey of St Denis are therefore all the more important, because they substantially add to our knowledge of this highest level of society.

37–40
35, 36

The present cathedral of Cologne is built over earlier Carolingian and Merovingian churches, and lies within the walls of the late Roman town. In 1959, during building activities under the choir, two rich graves were discovered, one of a Merovingian princess, the other of a six-year-old boy of equally high standing. Both were buried about the middle of the sixth century. The rich contents of the woman's grave and the full warrior's equipment found in the tomb of the boy suggest that both were members of the royal house. The fact that they were buried within the walls of one of the major churches of the time indeed makes this assumption almost a certainty. The capital of the eastern part of the

46

35 Four double-headed
serpents, looped into a
quatrefoil pattern, make
up this brooch from
Wittislingen

36 Large seventh-
century bow brooch with
radiating head from
Wittislingen, employing a
variety of goldsmith's
techniques, including
niello inlay on silver,
cloisonné garnets and
gold filigree

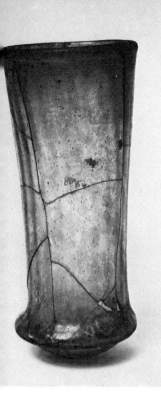

37–40 Finds from the early seventh-century tomb of a warrior at Morken. *Left*, his helmet, with an embossed strip decorated with stylized inhabited small ornament. *Above left*, a glass drinking cup. *Right*, a bronze shield boss, partly gilt. *Below*, a two-handled bronze dish

49

50

kingdom ruled by Clovis' grandson, Theodobert, had been at Rheims, but with the eastward expansion of the kingdom following the final conquest of Thuringia in 531 Cologne may well have become its major city.

The tomb of the princess was built of closely jointed staves, making a chamber 10 ft long and 2 ft 9 in. wide. The body was buried in a wooden coffin, the remaining area of the tomb being filled with grave goods which included six glass vessels and dishes, a bronze bowl, a wooden bucket *41* bound in gilded bronze and a small silver-mounted drinking horn. Within the coffin a rich array of gold jewellery was found, the most important pieces of which were a pair of ear-rings set with garnets, a pair of bow brooches and a pair *42* of rosette brooches, all decorated with cloisonné garnets and gold filigree. The rosette brooches have equal armed crosses on their raised centre bosses filled with a decoration of small circles of wire filigree. The princess's magnificent necklace is made up of seven gold-coin pendants, five splendid circular gold pendants decorated with very high quality filigree patterns and three shaped cloisonné garnet pendants – two of them of a shape that might be intended to represent royal cicadas of the kind found in Childeric's tomb. None of her rich garments survive, except for some fragments of hem worked in gold thread. From her thin leather belt, fastened by a heavy silver buckle, were suspended a small gold-handled knife, a gold-mounted crystal ball and an embossed silver container, perhaps for an amulet. The coins on her necklace and four more unmounted coins found in the tomb date the burial fairly exactly – the latest being a silver half *43* siliqua of the Ostrogothic king Athalaric (526–34), which would seem to place the time of the princess's death in the reign of Theodobert, in the second quarter of the sixth century.

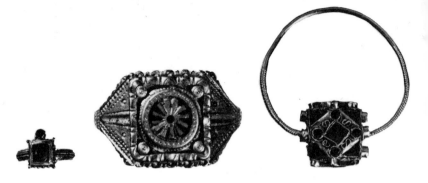

42 Jewellery from the sixth-century tomb of a Frankish princess excavated under Cologne Cathedral. *Above*, two finger-rings, and one of a pair of gold cloisonné ear-rings. *Below*, remains of a head-band woven with gold thread, set with a small jewelled stud, and one of a pair of circular brooches between a pair of gold cloisonné fibulae. It is interesting to note the slight variations of detailed design in the pair

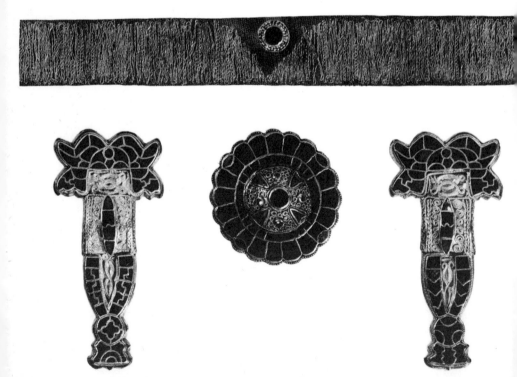

43 Plaited gold chain, with a pendant gold solidus of Theodosius II (408–50), from the tomb of the Cologne princess.

44 A group of glass vessels found in the sixth-century grave of a young warrior, excavated beneath Cologne Cathedral

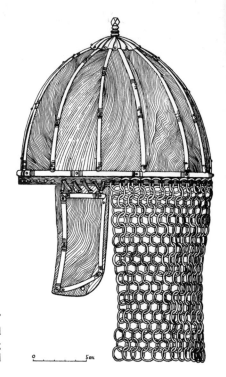

45 The child's version of the 'Spangenhelm'
type (Illus. 37), made of bronze-gilt strips and
horn plates, found in the sixth-century young
warrior's grave, below Cologne Cathedral

The young prince was also buried in a chamber, but one
built of stone slabs, his body lying on a wooden bier some
4 ft 7 in. long which can be fully reconstructed – a unique
survival of Frankish woodwork. At the foot of the bier
stood a small chair made of turned wood with a leather seat.
45 Slung on the back of the chair was a small helmet made of
gilt-bronze ribs and horn plates, with leather-lined horn
cheek-pieces and chain-mail neck protection – in short, a
child's version of the so-called 'Spangenhelm'. The weapons
found in the boy's grave were intended for an adult – a two-
edged long sword, two spears, a battle-axe, a bow with three
arrows and a large leather-covered shield with a central iron
44 boss. Bronze, glass and wooden vessels similar to those found
in the woman's grave were placed near the chair and a small
gold finger-ring was the boy's only personal adornment.

Perhaps the most interesting find in the tomb was a small turned wooden stick, some 20 in. long, placed by the boy's left side. Considering the ancestral weapons found in the tomb – so clearly fitting only to a boy of high rank – this stick may well be correctly interpreted as a royal sceptre.

Treasures of a Merovingian Queen

While these two important graves were excavated in Cologne, an undisturbed burial of perhaps even greater archaeological importance was unearthed from the crypt of the abbey church of St Denis near Paris, where the fifth-century St Genevieve had erected a church over the tomb of the third-century martyr St Dionysius. The abbey church has been a burial place of the Merovingian, Carolingian and medieval kings of France ever since. A large limestone coffin was found in which the remains of a female body, about forty years of age at the time of death, were discovered, with most of her magnificent costume still identifiable and an array of personal female jewellery unprecedented among Frankish burials. Laid on a bright red blanket or cloak, the *49, 50* body was dressed in a fine linen shift, over which she wore a knee-length tunic of violet silk. On her legs she wore stockings with crossed leather garters. The tunic was pulled in at the hips by an open-work gilt leather girdle, fitted with silver-gilt buckles and strap-ends. Over the tunic, an ankle-length dark-red silk gown completed her garments, with wide sleeves embroidered with gold thread at the cuffs. This gown, closed at the neck and at the waist by two superb circular gold brooches set with cloisonné garnets, was *47, 48* decorated by a magnificent large pin on the left breast, and *46* fell open below the waist. On her head, a red satin veil was fixed by two gold pins to her long blonde hair, then fell behind to the waist. Other jewellery included a pair of ear-rings, similar to the Cologne princess's ear-rings, while silver buckles and straps fitted with strap-ends fastened her leather slippers. In addition a very large nielloed belt-buckle, with a

46–48 A pair of gold cloisonné brooches and the top of the large cloak-pin, found in the tomb of Queen Arnegunde (*d.* about 570), excavated in the abbey church of St Denis, near Paris

49, 50 A plan of the finds in Queen Arnegunde's stone coffin, and an artist's reconstruction of the burial

plate and counter-plate decorated with gold and garnets, had been placed just above her waist. This large buckle is certainly from a man's belt, and may have been placed in the tomb as a burial gift. Of outstanding importance is a gold ring found on her hand, bearing the inscription ARNEGUNDIS (genitive of Arnegunde) around a monogram of the word REGINE.

Only one Frankish Queen Arnegunde is known to history, one of the consorts of Chlotar I, king of Soissons from 511 to 558 and sole king of the Franks from 558 to 561. According to Gregory of Tours, she was the sister of Chlotar's first wife, Ingunde, and Chlotar must have married her before 539, when Arnegunde's son Chilperic was born. We may assume, therefore, that she must have been born between about 520 and 525. The ring found on her finger is, of course, not conclusive evidence that it was she who was buried there. The ring is not a seal-ring and may have been a gift from the queen to someone close to her. However that may be, the date of the burial is not likely to be much later than about AD 570. Among the jewellery, a pair of small silver buckles and some strap-ends are archaeologically the most important.

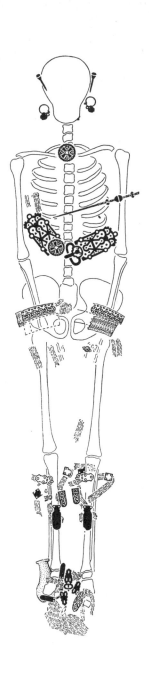
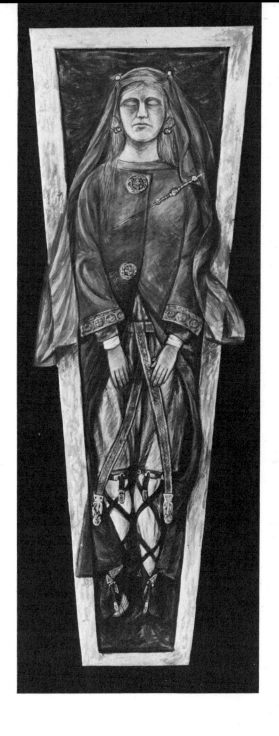

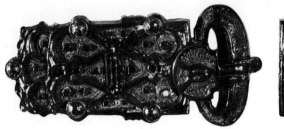

51, 52   *Above*, large buckle and counter-plate from a man's belt, probably placed in Arnegunde's tomb as a burial gift. *Opposite*, jewellery from her grave, including strap-ends and buckle, with interlaced and ribbon-animal decoration. The gold finger-ring is inscribed with ARNEGUNDIS (genitive of Arnegunde) around the monogram of REGINE

52   They are decorated with a style of animal art, very close to the one classified by Salin as 'Style II'. Instead of the fragmented animal art of Style I, in which parts of the bodies of creatures are broken up and re-assembled to form a pattern, in Style II, also called very aptly the 'ribbon animal' style, the bodies of the animals are elongated, intertwined and interlaced in a smooth and continuous, usually symmetrically arranged, pattern. It has been said that Style II found widespread use in northern Europe only after the beginning of the seventh century, and that it had been developed in north Italy as the result of the Lombardic invasion of Italy that took place in AD 568. At that time a new synthesis of Style I with older Mediterranean traditions of purely abstract banded interlace patterns is thought to have been created.

The appearance of something very like 'Style II' at the Frankish Court certainly no later than the 560's once again forces us to reconsider the origins and early history of Salin's Style II. Research in Sweden on important finds made after Salin's publication, especially at the great cemetery site of Valsgärde in Uppland, had already cast doubt on Salin's Style II (and Style III – a more elaborate and later development of Style II) being an adequate description of the variety of styles found in Scandinavia in the 'Vendel' period from

the late sixth to the end of the eighth century. In the publication of the Valsgärde finds we see animal art divided into five types and given the letters A to E; 'A' is said to form a link – or transition – between Salin's Style I and II; 'B' is meant to cover the broad definition of Salin's Style II, while C, D and E are different versions of both Salin's Style II and III, grouped under somewhat more precise definitions. The dating of this material is far from certain, but little of it is likely to date from before c. 600. One must also begin to wonder whether the archaeologist's attempts to group his styles by an analysis of detailed features of it, and drawing from such an analysis a chronological 'developmental' scheme, is supportable. More and more evidence seems to suggest that there are great areas of chronological overlap; in other words, that the animal styles of the Dark Ages, while they follow very broadly a chronological development, are not easily categorized, and many of its stylistic features are found in use at the same time. Perhaps the divisions of its styles depend more on the quality of the work and the patronage of different levels of society, or on direct contacts with distant areas, or a foreign workshop, as against indigenous development, than on any strictly chronological development.

53   Detail of an eighth-century silver-gilt bracteate pendant from Gotland, Sweden. The central design based, in the final analysis, on a Late Roman coin type, still retains something of the organic naturalism of the original, even at this late date. Indigenous traditions are also maintained – for example in the small human heads, used two centuries earlier in the gold collar from Västergotland (*Illus. 9*)

One suspects that the more fluid and continuous forms of the so-called 'Style II', as against the more broken patterns of the so-called 'Style I', may not all have originated in every region of Europe from a single source. Indeed, in Scandinavia, and for that matter in Britain, older, indigenous forms might have played at least a part in the development. The creatures found on the superb gold collars from Möne and Färjestaden, Västergotland, Sweden, for example, are usually dated to the early sixth century. Among them we find S-shaped or snake-like continuous bodies, usually set with granulations along their entire length, which come much closer to any definition of Style II than Style I, and are related to the kind of inter-laced animal forms also found on the gold 'bracteates' or imitation coins found in Denmark and in Britain in the fifth and sixth centuries. In such pieces, perhaps made for a more conservative and, as the use of gold would certainly suggest, richer section of society, one can still sense the forms of a more fluid, organic and fundamentally more naturalistic animal art connected with ancient Roman-Celtic traditions. In the bracteates these traditions are self-evident, as their types derive in the end from Roman coins. Can one see, therefore, in such very high-class work, a stream in strictly chronological terms contemporary with the so-called 'Style I', which sometimes merges with the more broken forms of Style I (in style 'A' for example), and which gains an ascendancy during the early sixth century, when, it is possible, influences from southern Europe also play a part?

In the case of the so-called 'Style II' strap-ends from Arnegunde's tomb, the symmetrical 'ribbon' style animals and the purer non-animal interlace found on another strap-

60

end may suggest no more than a knowledge of eastern Mediterranean patterns introduced into southern Gaul through growing monastic contacts, which can be found clearly in other arts besides those of the goldsmith. At much the same time similar influences are felt among the Langobardi (Lombards), both in their Pannonian homelands and, after 568, in the newly conquered areas of north Italy. To see the developments during the fifth and sixth centuries in this way may not have the advantage of a tidy, typologically defined chronology but it may be much nearer the intricacies of history.

The graves of Cologne and St Denis, then, provide the kind of information for the sixth century which the tomb of Childeric provided for the later fifth. By contrast with Childeric's tomb, it is clear that by the middle of the sixth century the more eclectic Germanic styles had fully penetrated the art of the court and the higher levels of aristocratic patronage. No longer was it necessary for the Frankish ruling families to rely on alien eastern tastes for their personal adornment and the decoration of their material goods. Out of crude beginnings, Germanic art of the *Reihengräber* civilization had, by the middle of the sixth century, fused with other elements and developed its truly aristocratic counterpart. Technically and artistically Merovingian secular art had come of age.

Chapter Four

The History of the Franks

The Saga of Chilperic and Brunhild

Although the archaeological material from cemeteries still remains a vital source of information of the age, it is no longer our only source. The growing power of Christianity and the Church, as well as the more settled and expanding nature of economic conditions in Europe, led to an increase in contacts with the Mediterranean world and its traditions, as well as to a fundamental broadening of the intellectual and cultural life of the Merovingian kingdom. The greatest historian of the 'Dark Ages', Gregory of Tours, lived at this time, born of an aristocratic Gallo-Roman family. At the age of eight his education was entrusted to his uncle, Gallus, bishop of Clermont. After entering the priesthood, he was elected bishop of Tours at the early age of thirty-three and consecrated in the year 573. Only two years later most of the first four books of his *History of the Franks* seem to have been written. Books five and six were probably composed in the early 580's and the final books, seven to ten ending in the year 591, were completed between *c.* 585 and the bishop's death in 594.

He writes in the preface of the first book as follows: 'In these times, when the practice of letters declines, nay, rather perishes in the cities of Gaul, there has been found no scholar trained in the art of ordered composition.' He goes on to affirm – with the usual modesty of early historians – his own inadequacies of learning and style of composition. Nevertheless he presents us, not only with detailed historical information not available from any other source, but with a vivid narrative and a rare sense of period, and especially a sense of the drama of human conflict, so much a part of his times.

After the death of Chlotar I in 561 a series of civil wars weakened the Merovingian royal house, wars made even more bitter by the family feuds that helped to cause them. Of the four sons of Chlotar I, one died six years after his father and, of the remaining three, Guntram, king of Orleans was content to hold the balance of power between the other two, Sigebert and Chilperic. Sigebert married Brunhild, a daughter of the king of the Visigoths and a woman of culture and education. His bride aroused the jealousy of his brother; he asked, and was granted, the hand of Brunhild's sister Galswintha. The marriage, however, did not prosper and he soon went back to a previous mistress, Fredegund. One morning Galswintha was found strangled in her bed. Political tension, now inflamed by personal vengeance, broke out in fierce war. Sigebert was victorious, but was murdered in the hour of triumph by two slaves sent by Fredegund with poisoned daggers.

The next ten years were spent in a struggle between Brunhild, governing in the name of her young son Childebert II, and Chilperic, now married to Fredegund. Both were outstanding personalities in an age not lacking in strength of character. Chilperic, 'the Nero and Herod of his time' according to Gregory of Tours, was a complex and interesting man – ruthless in ambition and driven on by insatiable greed, but a poet, a musician and an independent thinker in matters of religion. He admired Latin literature, introduced new letters into the German alphabet, and reformed the ancient Salic law in favour of women. Yet his rule was notorious for extortion and injustice, and at the bottom of his edicts he was in the habit of writing, 'Whoever disobeys this order shall have his eyes put out.' He was murdered in 584 as he returned from hunting.

Brunhild, a woman of indomitable will and qualities of high statesmanship, held her own for nearly thirty years against Chilperic's army, her own rebellious aristocracy and constant ill-fortune in the early deaths of her children and grandchildren. Her weapons were diplomacy, boldness and (when necessary) assassination, but she was also capable of surprising generosity – as when she sent back, unharmed, to Neustria an assassin sent by Fredegund to take her life. On the death of Guntram, king of Orleans, she easily annexed his kingdom to her own; she ruled over Austrasia and Burgundy, giving laws to laity and clergy alike, outliving her enemy Chilperic, her rival Fredegund, her own son, her grandsons, and great-grandsons. Finally, in 613, the united opposition of the Austrasian nobility (led by Arnulf of Metz and Pepin, the founders of the Carolingian family) achieved her downfall. She was tortured for three days; then, tied by the hair, one arm and one leg to a wild horse, she was dragged across rough ground until she died.

Mayors of the Palace

The new king of the whole of the Frankish dominions was Chlotar II, the son of Chilperic and Fredegund. Chlotar was succeeded by his son Dagobert in 629 who had already 54 reigned as king of Austrasia since 623. The Merovingian dynasty was already weak, undermined by strife of the kind just described. Dagobert, in a short but trenchant reign of ten years (629–39), combined the whole of the Frankish lands under his own rule. But even he, an unusually strong personality among the later Merovingian kings, was able to stem the flow against the Frankish royal house only for a time. The growing antagonism of the aristocracy – Dagobert complained that the nobles had robbed him of the best estates and domains in his kingdom – was too strong for the king to resist. The fact was that the kings of the early Middle Ages were able to maintain their power against their nobles only in a rapidly expanding kingdom – a condition that no longer existed by the middle of the sixth century, after Dagobert's reign.

54, 55   Gold coins of Dagobert (629–39) above, and of Charibert II (*d.* 630) below. The diadem profile portrait type is derived from imperial Roman gold solidi

The security of the supremacy of the royal house rested almost entirely on its superior wealth, for there was a need for an unremitting supply of new funds with which to pay for the loyalty of its followers. The constant division of this wealth among the sons of the king inevitably weakened the position of the rulers. Only as long as new territories were added to their royal domains by conquests, as in the time of Clovis and his immediate successors, was their position unassailable. Another difficulty, quite apart from their decline in personal ability in the quick succession of young and, on the whole, dissolute, vacillating and weak kings of the Merovingian dynasty, was the growing enmity between the more Romanized western and southern part of the kingdom. The western part was called Neustria – 'New Lands' – and the Germanic northern and eastern part was called Austrasia –

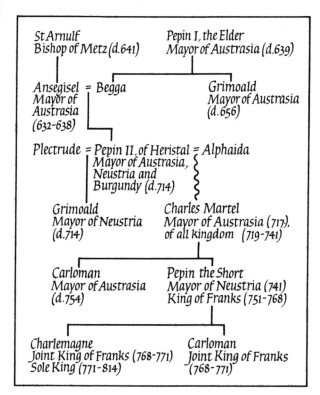

St Arnulf
Bishop of Metz (d. 641)

Pepin I, the Elder
Mayor of Austrasia (d. 639)

Ansegisel = Begga
Mayor of
Austrasia
(632-638)

Grimoald
Mayor of Austrasia
(d. 656)

Plectrude = Pepin II, of Heristal = Alphaida
Mayor of Austrasia,
Neustria and
Burgundy (d. 714)

Grimoald
Mayor of Neustria
(d. 714)

Charles Martel
Mayor of Austrasia (717),
of all kingdom (719-741)

Carloman
Mayor of Austrasia
(d. 754)

Pepin the Short
Mayor of Neustria (741)
King of Franks (751-768)

Charlemagne
Joint King of Franks (768-771)
Sole King (771-814)

Carloman
Joint King of Franks
(768-771)

56   The Arnulfian or, as it is more usually called, the Carolingian dynasty, down to Pepin the Short, who was crowned King of the Franks in 751. The ancestors of Charlemagne exercised their considerable power through the office of Mayor of the Palace

'East Lands' – names that first come into use in the late sixth century. In this struggle it was Austrasia which finally won supremacy. Not only were these 'East Lands', the Frankish homelands, more fully settled by Frankish peoples and therefore the basic source of strength in the Frankish kingdom, but also the course of history in the Mediterranean world made the final ascendancy of the area inevitable in the eighth century.

While the power of the Merovingian kings declined during the seventh century, that of the Mayors of the Palace, the leaders of the aristocracy, increased. Chlotar II and Dagobert had been forced to surrender most of their administrative authority to the landed nobility. Dagobert could impose himself by force of personality, and could intervene as king of the Franks in the politics of the Visigoths and Lombards. He was a wise judge, a patron of the arts and a friend of the Church. Even so, his power was severely limited. The country was divided into three semi-independent regions – Austrasia, Neustria and Burgundy. Each had its own laws, controlled by its own officials; the king could not appoint a nominee from outside. The great landowners in each region took it in turn to be Mayor of the Palace and their loyalties were naturally local rather than national.

After Dagobert the situation deteriorated. The later Merovingian kings mostly came to the throne as children and died in their twenties. They lived, surrounded by luxury, in country retreats, their names affixed to edicts and laws, but exercising no influence on the course of events. Yet such was the prestige of the blood royal that an attempt by Pepin's grandson Grimoald to assume the title of king was vigorously resisted; he was killed and the family that he represented went into the political wilderness for a generation.

Charles 'the Hammer'

Predictably, the Mayors of the Palaces of Neustria, Austrasia and Burgundy were at odds, and it was Austrasia, once more under the family of Pepin, which emerged as dominant. In 687 Pepin II (of Heristal), grandson of both Arnulf of Metz and Pepin I, defeated Berthar, Mayor of the Palace of Neustria, and from that date was effective ruler of nearly all the Merovingian kingdom. He died in 714 and was succeeded (after the usual internecine struggle) by his illegitimate son Charles – known as 'Martel', 'the Hammer'.

Charles was an able ruler and a military leader of genius. His unification of the country and ability to mobilize its resources came with the utmost opportuneness. In 719 he forced the last independent magnate, Eudo of Aquitaine, to acknowledge his suzerainty. The next year the Arabs crossed the Pyrenees.

They were held in check in the south for twelve years. Then in 732, under a new and fanatical leader, they took the field again and the tide of conquest that had begun nearly a century earlier in Arabia swept up the centre and west of France. Charles gathered an army and placed himself in a good strategic position at the confluence of the Clain and Vienne rivers. For seven days the two armies were encamped facing each other. Then in October 732 they joined battle – the Battle of Poitiers, or of Tours. It was the end of the Muslim expansion. Decisively beaten, they retreated again towards Spain. Avignon was liberated, and in alliance with Liutprand, king of the Lombards, Charles could now contain them in the south-west.

The Battle of Poitiers certainly ranks as one of the most critical in the history of the world, since the whole of European civilization can be said to have turned on its result. Charles' long-term victory, however, was not due entirely to his own efforts. The Moors might yet have rallied had they not, in their turn, become split by dissension. Their later attempts on Provence and Italy were firmly repulsed. At the same time Charles secured his frontier in the east. In 738 he defeated the Saxons and made them pay tribute, and it was he who enabled Boniface to carry out his evangelizing mission among the tribes of eastern Germany. He redistributed lands belonging to the Frankish Church, summoned assemblies and corresponded with the Pope. At the end of his reign the foundations had been laid upon which his son and grandson, Pepin and Charlemagne, were to build the new Carolingian empire.   56

All this while his official title was still 'Mayor of the Palace'. The curious constitutional fiction was preserved whereby the nominal ruler of the kingdom was always (apart from intervals when the throne was vacant) one or other of the effete *rois fainéants* of the exhausted Merovingian dynasty.

It was not until the reign of Pepin (Charles Martel died in 741) that the king in fact became king in name. At first Pepin shared the government with his brother Carloman. But in 747 Carloman renounced the world and entered a monastery.

Pepin sent an embassy to Rome, asking whether it were legitimate for him to assume the royal title. Pope Zacharius decided in his favour. In November 751 the last Merovingian, Childeric III, was formally deposed and Pepin annointed king of the Franks.

Chapter Five

The Frankish Church

The rise of the Mayors of the Palace was one feature of the seventh century. The other power to increase rapidly during this time, in spite of many temporary setbacks, was that of the Church, both in its secular branch under the bishops, and in its monastic branch. Although the spiritual life of the Frankish Church left much to be desired, the growing control exercised over it by Frankish aristocracy augmented its political power considerably. Early in the sixth century, at the Council of Orleans, only two bishops with Germanic names attended, while no less than thirty were drawn from the ranks of the older Gallo-Roman aristocracy; but by the early seventh century, at the Council of Paris, forty-one of the bishops present were of Germanic stock and only thirty-eight were of non-Germanic origin – many of them from the Christian East. These figures indicate both the growth of the Church and the infiltration of Frankish nobles into her ranks.

The growing power of the Church was the natural result of her tremendous expansion in wealth. Never were donations to the Church greater than in the Merovingian period. Her benefactors were many, not least among them the bishops themselves – drawn as they were from among the landed aristocracy. Bertram of Mans, for example, left no less than thirty-five estates to his see – and it must be remembered that all property acquired by the Church was inalienable. The Church also received other financial benefits, such as the exemption from custom dues and all sorts of taxes, while she herself was able to levy dues and tithes of many kinds. The Church always received, was never called

57 Map showing the growing number of
European monasteries and their attribution
from the late sixth to eighth centuries

up to 590
590 – 700
700 – 768

upon to pay out, and never had to divide her property among
a mass of heirs.

57   The monastic branch of the Church also expanded rapidly.
Some two hundred monasteries, mainly situated south of the
Loire, were in existence in the kingdom when St Columbanus,
the Irish missionary, arrived in Europe about the year 585.
His arrival seems to have opened the flood-gates to monastic
expansion, and in no other period in history were as many
monasteries founded as between the years 610 and 650 – the
saint himself having died at Bobbio in north Italy in 615. By
the end of the seventh century, well over four hundred
monasteries were in existence, and now spread over the
entire kingdom as far north as the river Meuse and as far east
as the upper Rhine. Some of the most famous monasteries of
the Middle Ages owe their foundation to this period, including Prüm, Moyenmontier, Malmédy, Stavelot and
St Gall.

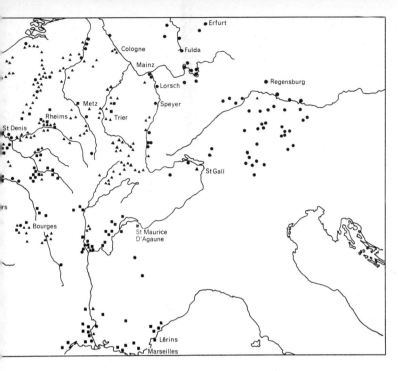

Art in the Service of God

It was, of course, inevitable that expansion in wealth and power on this scale resulted in a parallel expansion of cultural output. Artistic influences from a wider background began to enrich the repertoire of Frankish art. Although pitifully little survives of early monastic art in the Merovingian kingdom, that little plainly shows these new influences at work – influences from the older centres of culture, from Italy, from Byzantium and especially from Syria and Egypt, the birthplace of monasticism itself.

Already in the sixth century, precise instances of such direct influences can be cited. When Chlotar I repudiated his wife Radegund, she founded the monastery of St Croix at Poitiers and became its first abbess. In the year 569, she asked the Byzantine emperor Justin II for a fragment of the Holy Cross, that precious relic kept at Jerusalem which had been discovered by St Helena in the fourth century in a cave near the site of Our Lord's Crucifixion. Her wish was granted and

73

58 Reliquary of St Croix, Poitiers, containing a fragment of the True Cross sent by Justin II to St Radegund. The enamelled central panel survives, but the wings are known only from an eighteenth-century drawing

58   still today the convent of St Croix preserves a fragment of the Cross, mounted in a gold reliquary panel, decorated with cloisonné enamel and set with garnets and green pastes in rectangular cells surrounding the relic and framing the panel. In the French Revolution, the reliquary lost its two side wings, which are known only from an eighteenth-century drawing. Documentary evidence of Radegund's acquisition of the relic is undisputed, but some scholars believe that the golden reliquary itself cannot be of as early a date as 569, and attribute it to a Byzantine workshop of the eleventh or even the twelfth century. Yet it is no easier to find designs similar to its decorative scroll work in these later centuries than it is in the sixth century. Also, it is difficult to understand how the relic could have received a later Byzantine framework while in the possession of the convent at Poitiers. St Radegund's so-*59, 60*   called reading desk also shows East Christian features, while quite a number of objects of East Christian origin have been

74

59, 60   St Radegund's wooden reading desk preserved at her convent in Poitiers.
Almost certainly a gift from the East, it has in the centre the Lamb with the four
evangelist symbols in the corners

61, 62 Seventh-century Frankish iron buckle
and counter-plate with silver and copper inlay.
The origin of the so-called Style II interlaced
ornament remains controversial, but fifth-
century Coptic textiles, such as the one illustrated
above, may well have played a part in
transmitting Eastern Mediterranean ornamental
conventions to western Europe

63 Trade contacts with Egypt are proved by a
number of Coptic imports found in the West,
such as this bronze bowl found near Mainz.
Such bowls were sometimes imitated, see, for
example, the somewhat rudimentary bowl found
at Morken (*Illus. 40*)

brought to light during the excavation of sixth- and seventh-century sites, especially in the Rhineland and south-western Germany. Imports from Coptic Egypt have also been found in Britain and north Italy.

Clearly, we can assume that in a similar way, either by direct trade or by contacts through the monastic connections with the Middle East, other materials also found their way to north-western Europe. Such imports must have included textiles, decorated with abstract as well as pictorial patterns of the kind known from Egyptian burials, ivory carvings, metalwork and pottery. Indirect evidence of such imports is plentiful. The interlace patterns found on bronze buckles and strap-ends, and on the Frankish iron buckles and counter- 61, 62 plates inlaid with silver, so popular in the seventh century, are found most frequently on the decorative roundels and strips on Coptic textiles. East Christian ivory carvings are known to have been in Europe since the early Middle Ages. Some of these carvings were to be copied in Carolingian times, others, like the famous reliefs now in Charlemagne's church at Aachen, were built into a medieval pulpit as early as the eleventh century and may have been imported into Europe long before that.

Among the stone carvings to have survived from the seventh century, the tomb slab of Bishop Boethius of Carpentras, who died in 604, provides us with an interesting example of such indirect evidence. Carved on the slab is a cross, which has the *Alpha* and *Omega* suspended from its arms by small chains. This is clearly copied from a metal altar-cross, because the position of the first and the last letters of the Greek alphabet, which symbolize the Beginning and the End, are reversed on the stone carving and were obviously copied from the wrong side of a metal prototype. A number of bronze altar-crosses of the sixth century that survive from Coptic Egypt show us the kind of object that the Frankish mason must have copied.

64

65

64, 65 *Left*, stone tomb slab of Bishop Boethius of Carpentras (*d*. 604). *Right*, Coptic bronze altar-cross, probably sixth century

66–68 *Top left*, the fragment from a choir screen from the church of St Peter, Metz, is basically in a sub-Roman tradition and perhaps of seventh-century date. Although such a tradition might be derived from early Christian models in Gaul (*below*), a more immediate contact with contemporary Coptic sculpture (*top right*) is also possible. Recent research suggests yet a third alternative, namely that the style resulted from renewed contact with northern Italy in the later eighth or early ninth century. *Below*, an early Christian sarcophagus from Gaul, now in the Toulouse Museum, with the Fall of Man on the end panel, and scenes including the Raising of Lazarus and the Sacrifice of Isaac on the front

One element in the Boethius slab not mentioned so far –
the upper part, carrying an inscription on a classical tabula
with a pointed architectural pediment above – could not
have been derived from an imported piece of metalwork, but
is strictly in the monumental classical tradition. In the
Boethius slab this may well be copied from Gallo-Roman
sculpture which survived into the seventh century in large
quantity in France. No such source could account for the few
fragments of sculpture from the church of St Peter at Metz.
One of these fragments, which shows a standing saint between columns supporting a pediment, is undoubtedly   *66*
derived from East Christian monastic art, probably from that *67*
of Coptic Egypt. Other Metz fragments, carved with interlace patterns, vine-scrolls and plants issuing from two-
handled vases, equal-armed crosses and architectural motifs,
all point to exactly the same source. Only the addition of
animal heads to the ends of the strands of interlace betray the
Germanic carvers. Unfortunately the date of the carvings is
not certain. The church of St Peter was probably founded
early in the seventh century – the dates 613 or 620 have been
suggested. The fragments themselves show that they were
not part of the architectural structure but were most probably
part of a choir screen. Certainly a date towards the middle of
the seventh century, during the period of rapid monastic
expansion, would seem to be entirely acceptable.

Among the archaeological finds, reflections of this kind of
direct Mediterranean influence can also be seen. The motif
of an equestrian figure, often holding a lance, found on the *69, 70*
pierced bronze decorative discs discovered frequently in
Frankish graves, is thought to have been inspired by the
equestrian saints so often represented in the Christian East.
The famous gold disc-brooch from Pliezhausen is probably *71*
derived from similar sources, though in this case it may have
been transmitted through north Italy. A popular type of
Burgundian bronze buckle, with a rectangular plate decorated
with Christian subjects such as Daniel in the Lions' Den, or

69, 70   The charging horseman is another
familiar Merovingian motif that can be traced
back to Eastern prototypes. *Above*, a Coptic
textile roundel from Akhmin and, *below*, the
stone funerary stele from Hornhausen of
c. AD 700

82

71–73 *Above*, the gold disc-brooch from
Pliezhausen; *right*, a decorative bronze disc from
a Frankish grave, and *below*, a bronze-gilt plaque,
probably of Lombard origin, from Stabio in
Switzerland. All are of early seventh-century date

74–78   Daniel in the Lion's Den is another very popular Frankish theme, which may derive, in its pictorial form, from a number of sources. The St Calentius sarcophagus (*c.* 620) (*opposite, centre*) illustrates a straightforward representation of the scene, while the Burgundian buckle plates (*opposite, below*) may reflect a more ancient Germanic tradition of the 'Man between Beasts', which is also behind the Frankish pierced sixth-century plaque (*opposite, above*). The Burgundian buckle *above*, however, may be connected with the scene of St Menas between his Camels, known in the West from imported pilgrim's flasks (*Illus. 79*) and here re-interpreted as Daniel. The form of the buckle itself is based on a Late Roman model, like the ivory buckle of St Caesarius (470–542) from the tomb at Arles (*below*)

79, 80 Sixth-century ivory pyx, probably from Alexandria, with St Menas, and *left*, a cruder but contemporary representation of the same saint on a pottery pilgrim's bottle

pairs of birds facing a central vase, can also be shown to have been derived from well-established East Christian models. The Daniel scene, especially, looks very similar indeed to a

79   common type of pottery flask given to pilgrims at the shrine of St Menas near Alexandria, on which St Menas is represented between two camels, which kneel to the saint. The indistinct modelling of these simple flasks could easily have been re-interpreted to represent the more popular and better-known subject of Daniel in the Lions' Den. In a series of Christian tombstones carved in the Rhineland in the seventh century we find a number that show the same strong eastern

81   influence. Perhaps a stone from Gondorf is the most outstanding example of this trend. Not all the tombstones show quite so much Mediterranean influence, however. That from

81   Tombstone or panel from a choir screen from Gondorf on the Moselle. Seventh century

82–84 The mid–seventh–century tombstone from Niederdollendorf combines pagan with Christian iconography. The warrior (*left*) is shown with grave-goods and combing his hair, believed to be a symbol of the continuation of the forces of life. The other side of the same stone (*left, below*) shows what is thought to be Christ – certainly a nimbed figure, but most unusually carrying a spear. The same kind of Germanic and Christian mixture, in both style and iconography, is also seen in the powerful stone from Moselkern (*below*)

Niederdollendorf bears a full-length figure, probably in- 82, 83 tended to represent Christ with rays emanating to form a kind of mandorla – a total halo, with a fragment of interlace below. The representation on the other side shows the deceased carrying a sword and combing his hair, to symbolize the continuation of the forces of life, while the forces of darkness are shown by two snakes, one double-headed. By his side, his grave goods are indicated by a pilgrim's flask. The mere fact that representational art was attempted at all suggests Mediterranean influence, but, both in content and style, the Germanic elements predominate here. The power- ful stone from Moselkern, pierced with two crosses, a diagonal 84 cross below and a Christian cross above, appears at first sight to be an entirely original creation completely in keeping with the abstract taste of the northern peoples. Closer inspection, however, reveals the figure of the crucified Saviour, with a halo decorated with three small crosses on the upper cross. This again points clearly to a Mediterranean source, although it is obvious that any such model has here been re-created in an astonishingly original form. In the Moselkern tombstone, the Frankish carver has taken alien sources and made use of them and, after fully absorbing them, created a thoroughly Frankish art form.

Craftsmanship in Gold

Much the same creative absorption and adaptation of alien influences can be seen in another category of object popular in the Merovingian kingdom in the seventh century – the large gold disc-brooches, this time achieved by Frankish goldsmiths. More than forty such brooches have been found so far, varying in size from about $1\frac{1}{2}$ to 3 in. in diameter. They are made of a bronze base, on which the pin is mounted, overlaid by a thin sheet of gold on the front which is decorated with gold-wire filigree and set with gems or glass pastes. The majority of them have been found in the Middle Rhine area, between Bonn and Coblenz.

85–88 *Above left*, a seventh-century circular brooch found
in the Rhineland at Minden, near Trier, modelled in design
and technique on a north Italian type of the kind shown,
above right, from Castel Trosino. *Below*, the same type of
brooch, from Kärlich, making use of Germanic animal
ornament and, *opposite*, a late and very splendid example of
this category, found at Mölsheim. Mounted in the centre
of the very popular quatrefoil design is a Roman cameo

Both in structure and design, this group of brooches differs
remarkably from the traditional Germanic brooches. Although their circular form and the use of filigree combined
with symmetrically arranged gems can be found in earlier
Frankish brooches, yet their total effect is very different. The
quatrefoil shape employed in some of them is a new form and
the settings of gems, in a kind of gold box with a broad frame,
are a new form for Frankish goldsmiths. Undoubtedly, this
form of setting is of Byzantine origin. Also, the fact that
circular brooches of somewhat similar design and with
filigree – though rarely set with simple, great settings of
gems – have been found in Lombard north Italy, especially at
86 Castel Trosino, strongly suggests that these brooches were

inspired by influences from that area. Here the Byzantine traditions were firmly rooted in the area around Ravenna, which had been under the direct control of the Byzantine emperors until the later sixth century. However strong the Mediterranean influences were on these brooches, Frankish goldsmiths fully absorbed them and created an unmistakably Frankish type. In two of them, one found at Kärlich and the other at Kettig, even Germanic animal ornament, consisting of large beaked bird heads, was successfully absorbed into the design. This ornament enables us to date these two brooches to the first half of the seventh century; others are also dated to the seventh century by the contexts in which they were found. Perhaps the most magnificent example, found at

87

88 Mölsheim, of quatrefoil shape, and set with a fine antique cameo gem in the centre, is among the latest of the series. In its severe, precise structure we begin to see elements of the more self-conscious revival of classical forms which might suggest an early Carolingian date for the brooch – certainly one must date it well after the year 700.

As a whole, however, these brooches show most strikingly the broadening of the cultural base in the Merovingian kingdom of the seventh century. They illustrate a period in which Frankish craftsmen were no longer restricted to their Germanic heritage, and in which they were able to absorb alien influences, especially those of the Mediterranean world, and re-interpret them creatively.

The Monastic World

In all this we have seen the first effects of the expansion of Frankish art under the influence of the growing wealth in the country as a whole, and in the Church in particular. As has been said before, secular art, or more exactly, the full evidence we gain from the Germanic burial customs, dies out early in the eighth century. But to replace it, we have the development of Christian art, under the patronage of the Church,

89 beginning about the middle of the seventh century, and growing rapidly from that time on to dominate the picture we have of art in the Frankish kingdom. We have seen the influence of the eastern Mediterranean, and we have suggested that it was the result of the close ties that must have existed between the new monastic Church in France and the older monasticism of the eastern Mediterranean that inspired it. Such a monastic culture was to be the basis of post-classical Christian culture in western Europe. It was concerned from the first with far more than only the visual arts – its aim was the preservation of learning in the widest sense. The arts of literature, history, rhetoric, grammar, and astronomy, as well as the study of the scriptures and the writings of the Fathers of the Church were included in its orbit – a culture of far

89   A seventeenth-century drawing of the so-called Chalice of St Elegius, made for the abbey of Chelles, probably early seventh century. The original was destroyed during the French Revolution. If this cup is indeed a chalice, it represents the application to the production of altar vessels of a goldsmith technique hitherto mainly employed in creating personal jewellery

wider and deeper significance than that depending on the merely material riches of court life. This form of monastic culture saw its beginnings in north-western Europe in the period of monastic expansion in the first half of the seventh century. In the far north, in a fusion of the religious zeal of the ascetic Irish monks, the skill of Germanic craftsmen and the humanist learning of the classical world introduced into Britain by the Roman mission of St Augustine, a monastic culture was created that stands alone as the greatest single achievement in Europe before the Carolingian renaissance of the early ninth century.

In a more modest way, however, and at exactly the same time, the Frankish Church began to take the first steps towards an understanding of culture in the same, broad sense. The most outstanding figure in this cultural expansion – and its very beginning – Bishop Gregory of Tours, has been mentioned already. In England, St Augustine arrived at Canterbury in 597. The *scriptoria* at Lindisfarne, Monkwearmouth and Jarrow laid the foundations for their great works at the end of the seventh century, while the first mag-

90 nificent high crosses were being carved at Bewcastle and at
91 Ruthwell. But it was the Merovingian kingdom that saw the earliest richly illuminated manuscripts to have come down to us being written and the remarkable sarcophagi at Jouarre being carved.

The abbey of Notre Dame of Jouarre had been founded in about AD 630 by Adon, brother of St Ouen. Of the main buildings of the abbey nothing remains, but to the north of them, in the area of the abbey's cemetery, parts of two
92–95 funerary crypts survive. Nineteenth-century excavations on their site have shown that the crypts, now joined together, were originally the crypts of two churches built alongside each other; that to the north is dedicated to St Paul, the other to St Ebrigisile. The sculptured details of the latter, especially the capitals, look later than the seventh century – a date as late as the ninth or even tenth century is likely. The marble
95 capitals of the crypt of St Paul, however, belong to a group characteristic of the seventh century, believed to have been the work of a school of sculptors based on Aquitaine. The alterations made at this time to the church of St Jean at Poitiers, a building mentioned earlier, included the addition of a number of very similar marble capitals, while others are

94

90, 91 The Bewcastle (*left*) and Ruthwell crosses illustrate the high quality of decorative and figurative carving achieved in Britain *c.* A D 700, soon after the creation, in the Merovingian kingdom, of sculpture of comparable quality (as at Jouarre, *Illus. 97*)

92, 93 *Above*, the crypt of St Ebrigisile, abbey of Notre Dame, Jouarre and *below*, a part of the west wall of the crypt of St Paul. It shows high-quality masonry, laid in various patterns, and proves the existence, as early as the seventh century, of a tradition which was still used as late as the ninth, in Carolingian buildings such as the gate-house of Lorsch Abbey

94, 95　A general view of the early crypt of St Paul, abbey of Notre Dame, Jouarre, with the sarcophagus of Theodochilde (*d.* about 662) on the right and that of Bishop Agilbert (*d.* about 685) on the left. *Below*, in detail, two of the beautifully carved marble capitals of the crypt of St Paul, showing the persistence of late antique forms in the seventh century, probably carved in Aquitaine

96 The sarcophagus of the first abbess of Jouarre, Theodochilde, the niece of
the founder. She died soon after 662. The crisp carving of the sides, decorated
with a repeated pattern of a shell motif, is in marked contrast to the lid originally
decorated with elaborate scrolls, now badly weathered, and therefore almost
certainly separated from the sarcophagus for part of its history

known for example at Moissac, St Philibert de Grandlieu, St Denis and St Pierre de Montmartre. The whole group shows carving of a surprising degree of skill in the handling of imperial Roman traditions at such a late date, although the free and exotic way Roman motifs are used differentiates them at once from the more restrained forms of the late Roman capital we have seen from La Daurade at Toulouse. The vaulting of the roof of the present crypt is, naturally, of later date, although the disposition of the original columns makes it clear that a groined vault is likely to have been part of the original structure. The west wall, with its very fine diaper patterns in carefully cut stone, interrupted by slim buttresses or wall arcading, may also well be part of the original late seventh-century building. Such masonry would certainly confirm the Venerable Bede's high opinion of the skill of Frankish masons. The very simple patterns at Lorsch Abbey in Germany may well have been derived from a Frankish tradition of this kind which, in the end, goes back to Roman models. It may also be worth while to mention in this context the pedimented triangular window heads at St Jean at Poitiers, probably also added in the seventh century, which look so similar to the triangular heads of the external Lorsch arcade on the first floor. Perhaps here, too, the Carolingian builders were drawing on Frankish traditions. Unfortunately, far too little evidence survives, however, to do justice to the role Frankish architecture is likely to have played as a source for the Carolingian period.

The Sarcophagi of Jouarre

In addition to the unique fragments of seventh-century architecture at Jouarre, the crypt contains a number of stone sarcophagi, at least two of which are of outstanding interest. The earlier of the two is the sarcophagus of the first abbess of *96* Jouarre, Theodochilde, the niece of the founder, who died soon after A D 662. Both sides of the sarcophagus are decorated with two rows of crisply carved sea shells, with three lines of beautifully cut inscription above, between and below these rows. The steep ridge roof now on the sarcophagus, once decorated with splendid large circles of foliate scrolls of very different character, is in a poor state of preservation, which suggests that it must at some time have been separated from the tomb. Although the decoration of this sarcophagus, especially the shells on its sides, are no doubt fundamentally of Late Roman and probably eastern origin, nothing that can account for the remarkable design as a whole has ever been put forward. But the broad, flat bands with inscription remind one somewhat of the similar inscribed broad flat frames around the figure sculpture of the Ruthwell Cross in Britain – a work which may date from about the same time. The rather thick and simplified figure sculpture of the same cross should also be compared to a very similar treatment of the figure in relief on the second sarcophagus at Jouarre, that of Bishop Agilbert, who died probably soon after his retirement to Jouarre in 685. Agilbert, of Frankish birth and a brother of Theodochilde, is known to have gone to Britain and preached in Wessex about the year 650. He later became bishop of the West-Saxons at Winchester, and took part in the famous Synod of Whitby in 664. Here he and Bishop Wilfred led the party that supported the Roman faction in the Anglo-Saxon Church against the Irish party in the dispute about the annual fixing of the date of Easter. Later, he returned to France and became bishop of Paris in 668.

97, 98

His sarcophagus is even more remarkable than that of his sister Theodochilde. On its long side, which decreases in height from the head-end, is a seated figure of Christ on a throne holding an unfurled scroll in his left hand. To each side of him a number of standing figures are carved, their arms raised in the early Christian pose of prayer. The damaged condition of the sculpture makes it difficult to be certain, but there seem to be six such figures on each side, probably representing the choir of the Apostles flanking the Throne. At the head of the coffin, invisible in its present position in a cramped

97

98

97, 98 *Above*, the side of the sarcophagus of Bishop Agilbert, who died soon after 685, and *below*, the head of the same sarcophagus (photograph of a cast) showing a Christ in Majesty with the four symbols of the Evangelists. This sarcophagus is one of the very rare survivals of seventh-century figure carving, comparable in quality to the series of high crosses carved in Britain from the late seventh century onwards (*Illus. 90, 91*)

99, 100 *Above*, the fifth-century mosaic in the apse of the church of St David in Salonica, with a Christ in Majesty between the four evangelist symbols, showing the same rare composition of this scene (with the four beasts partly hidden behind Christ's mandorla) as the head of Agilbert's sarcophagus. *Opposite*, folio 132 v of the Sacramentary of Gelasius, written about 750 near Paris, perhaps at Chelles. The ornamental vocabulary, almost entirely of Eastern Mediterranean forms, especially fishes and birds, is used on the page with an emphasis on larger motifs at the beginning, diminishing in size as the text progresses, first developed in Hiberno-Saxon art

niche of the crypt, a Christ in Majesty is known to be carved, in a mandorla supported by the four apocalyptic symbols of the Evangelists – the angel of St Matthew, the eagle of St John, the lion of St Mark and the bull of St Luke. The particular form of this composition, in which the symbols seem to be half hidden behind the mandorla, again points to East Christian models, where it appears both in Egypt in the sixth- to seventh-century wall-painting at Bawit and in the
99 apse mosaic of the church of Hosios David at Salonica, a Byzantine church of the fifth century.

IN NO MI NE

DNI NRI IHU

XPI SALUATO

INCIPIT LIBER

SACRAMENTORUM ROMANAE,

aeclesiae ordinis anni circuli

ORATE ET PRAECES

Merovingian Manuscripts – the Unique Synthesis

One of the earliest manuscripts to survive from the Frankish kingdom is now preserved in the Cathedral Library of Cologne (No. 212). It was probably written in the south of France, perhaps at Lyons towards the middle of the seventh century – just a little earlier than the earliest Northumbrian manuscripts to have come down to us. But whereas the northern manuscripts of that period are largely decorated with patterns taken directly from the Germanic goldsmiths' workshops, together with some that reflect earlier Irish traditions, the Frankish manuscript draws entirely on Late Roman motifs and contemporary eastern ornament. The small bird pecking at a bunch of grapes, incorporated into the initial 'D' on folio 123 B, could inhabit almost any Mediterranean work of eastern decorative art, whether in stone, mosaic or painting. But it was not until the first half of the eighth century that Merovingian illumination was fully to develop its characteristic style. We can study this style in the 'Gothic Missal' in the Vatican Library (Reg. Lat. 317) of *c.* AD 700, probably from the monastery of Luxeuil; in the 'Chronicle of Fredegar' in the Bibliothèque National, Paris (Lat. 10910) of *c.* AD 715, possibly painted in eastern France; in the Sacramentary of Gelasius), written *c.* 750 near Paris, perhaps at *100–102* Chelles, and now in the Vatican Library (Reg. Lat. 316); and in the 'Gundohinus Gospels' now in the Town Library at *107, 108* Autun (MS 3), written at Fleury between 751 and 754. The colours of this style are bright and gay, its drawing lively and rapid, almost part of the written word on the page rather than a decorative addition. The illuminators made extensive use of the compass and the ruler to create their patterns. Human figures appear rarely, but animals, birds and especially fishes, often used to construct the larger lettering itself, were spread in rich profusion over the pages. What at first sight often seems to be crude and barbaric, is in fact in its total effect handled with dash and skill and achieves a kind of sophisticated, brittle elegance.

102 This page faces the folio reproduced earlier (*Illus. 100*) in the Sacramentary of Gelasius. The Cross has an Agnus Dei in the centre and the letters Alpha and Omega, the 'Beginning and the End', are suspended from its arms. The arch under which it is placed is supported on marble columns, carried on bases decorated with addorsed animals

103, 104 Details of two pages from the Sacramentary of Gellone, probably also written and decorated at the abbey of Chelles near Paris, towards the end of the eighth century. *Above*, smaller initials from the manuscript are shown: a fish has escaped from the letter 'D' of which it formed a part and is being sternly pinned back by a hand holding a fork. The female figure, *below*, makes the letter 'A'. She carries a censer in her right hand and a small cross in the left – objects of this kind and of this shape are commonly found in the Christian east. The blocks of lettering, the key pattern both on some of the letters and on the dress of the figure, and the red dots surrounding the letters indicate that Insular art was also known to the illuminator

105 A marginal drawing of Christ in Majesty, perhaps unfinished, in the Chronicle of Fredegar (Paris, Bibl. Nat., lat. 10910), dating from the mid-eighth century. The style of the figure may be compared to the sub-Roman tradition illustrated opposite

106 Carved stone altar of King Ratchis (744–49) at Cividale in northern Italy, set up in memory of his father, Duke Pemmo of Friuli, shows a Christ in Majesty, flanked by seraphs, carried in a mandorla by four flying angels

The origins of this singular style, so different from the per-
fection and metallic precision of the Germanic ornament that
controls much of the Anglo-Saxon style of the period, has
aroused much controversy among students. Most commonly,
scholars point to Coptic and Armenian manuscripts, where a
very similar vocabulary of forms is to be found – although all
the books that can be cited are later in date than the eighth
century. Scholars who adhere to this thesis have to argue
that earlier books in this style existed in the East, but have not
survived. Others claim that the style was first developed in
the Merovingian kingdom itself. Whatever the truth may be,
the parts that make up the forms of Merovingian illumination
are undoubtedly derived from the broad stream of eastern
influences to which we have constantly to refer – mixed in the
manuscripts with much that is derived from the Lombard art
of north Italy. In the figure style in particular, Italy may well
have provided the most important sources. We need only
compare the drawing of a 'Christ in Majesty' in the Fredegar   *105*
manuscript in Paris, with the stone altar carved at Cividale   *106*

107, 108   Two pages from the Gundohinus Gospels, written at Fleury between 751 and 754 (Autun, Bibl. Mun., MS. lat. 3). *Below*, detail of the evangelist St Matthew and *opposite*, the page with Christ in Majesty, between the four evangelist symbols. An example of the continuing tradition of Mediterranean figural art in the Frankish kingdom

109, 110 *Opposite*, a decorative page, showing an acceptance of quite intricate Insular interlace, from a Commentary of St Jerome, now in Paris (Bibl. Nat., lat. 11627). *Above*, the opening folio of the abridged *History of the World* by Orosius, preserved at Laon (Bibl. Mun., MS 137). Orosius, a Spanish priest, was encouraged to write his history by St Augustine

between 737 and 744, to be convinced of this. Another element that points to Italy is to be found in a book attributed to the *scriptorium* of Laon, now in Paris (Lat. 12168), dating from *c.* AD 770. On folio Cb, the two columns that support the arch are carried on the backs of lions – an architectural form derived from classical antiquity that was so well known in Italy that it led to a revival of it in the architecture of the Romanesque period there. It should be mentioned, too, that the animals on this page with interlaced legs and tails show that Anglo-Saxon illumination was not unknown at Laon either. Merovingian illumination continued well on into the later eighth century. The ornamental details employed in some schools, at Tours, for example, under the great British scholar Alcuin, even lasted on into the Carolingian period of the early ninth century. This in spite of the great and very different schools of illumination created by the patronage of the emperor Charlemagne in the late eighth century.

111, 112 *Left,* the Porta della Pescheria, Modena Cathedral, early twelfth century and *opposite,* a decorative page from St Augustine's Commentary of the first seven books of the Bible, mid-eighth century, probably written at Laon (Aisne) (Paris, Bibl. Nat., lat. 12168). The interlaced animals show strong Insular influence, but the columns carried on the backs of lions is an ancient Roman motif, which again became very popular in the Romanesque architecture of Italy

Relics of the Saints

The monastic workshops of the early eighth century also produced works of art other than illuminated manuscripts. The techniques learned in the development of secular goldsmiths' work, and perfected in such jewellery as the Wittislingen fibula, began to be put at the service of the Church. Altar vessels, covers decorated in gold, silver and jewels for the fine illuminated books, altar frontals and reliquaries were made to glorify and decorate the House of God. Unfortunately, most of these things are known to us only from inadequate contemporary descriptions – it is only natural that objects made in precious materials are prone to looting in times of war, to be melted down in times of need and to be refashioned to accord with changes of taste and fashion.

The great increase in the popularity of relics, especially among the Irish missionaries, resulted in the production of large quantities of precious reliquaries to house the sacred remains. Relatively few though they are in number, more of these have come down to us because the reverence they commanded tended to improve their chances of survival. Probably the finest among them is the reliquary donated by the priest Theuderich to the church of St Maurice d'Agaune in southern Switzerland. The donation is recorded in an inscription on the back of the little shrine, which is fitted with hinged strap-ends on the sides to enable it to be carried on a leather strap. The steep roof, the sides and the front are decorated with gold cloisonné inlay of garnets, pastes and pearls. Larger gem-stones and late antique intaglio gems are attached to the surface in settings of the kind we have found on the disc-brooches discussed earlier. In the centre of the front of the reliquary is mounted a glass paste cameo in classical taste, of a kind that has been shown to be of north Italian origin and of eighth-century date. Although this type of reliquary is normally described as 'house-shaped', it would be more correct to see the origin of this shape in the kind of sarcophagi we have seen at Jouarre – a miniature funerary monument in which the sacred relics were laid to rest. The 116 style of the inlayed decoration would seem to be quite in keeping with eighth-century jewellery found in the Alamannic area of the Frankish kingdom in which the abbey of St Maurice is situated, although some scholars have preferred to attribute this reliquary to a Burgundian workshop.

Another superb little reliquary, of much the same general shape and also fitted with strap-ends on the sides, is the Warnebertus reliquary in the Treasury of the Collegiate 113 Church at Beromünster in Switzerland. Cast in gilt-bronze, it is enriched with coloured inlay and decorated with typical ribbon-style animal ornament on the front, and foliage and scroll patterns of Byzantine origin on the back. Another small reliquary of very similar type, and perhaps from the same workshop, was found on the Rhine near Nymegen and 115 is now preserved in the Archbishop's Museum at Utrecht. It is difficult to say where in the Frankish kingdom these reliquaries might have been made. The knowledge of both Germanic animal ornament and Byzantine ornament – the latter probably filtered into the Frankish area through north Italy – was available in most parts of the kingdom.

In the nature of their ornament these reliquaries show clearly that the craftsmen who had been responsible for the secular buckles, strap-ends and brooches were beginning to be drawn into the service of the Church. Indeed, the Church was drawing mainly on the styles available in secular Germanic art, but in a small shrine of St Mummole in the 114 abbey church of Fleury (St Benoît-sur-Loire), decoration far closer to the East Christian styles we have seen in the manuscripts is employed. Linked rosettes appear below, some filled with equal-armed crosses, while on the steep roof a row of six standing figures, probably Apostles, appear under an arcade. The resemblance this decoration bears to manuscript illumination of the early eighth century shows that the other monastic arts were now beginning to turn to similar East Christian sources. The large reliquary casket, decorated with

113, 114 *Above*, the St Warnebertus reliquary in the Treasury of the collegiate church at Beromünster, Switzerland. Bronze-gilt, inlaid with garnets, probably from the same workshop as the Nymegen reliquary (*Illus. 115*). *Below*, the small house-shaped reliquary of St Mummole, abbey church of Fleury (St Benoît-sur-Loire), decorated in embossed bronze-gilt with six saintly figures on the roof

115, 116   Another two portable reliquaries, in the shape of miniature sarcophagi. *Above*, bronze-gilt, inlaid with garnets, found near Nymegen, now in the Archbishop's Museum, Utrecht and, *below*, perhaps the finest of the surviving examples, now in the Treasury of St Maurice d'Agaune, Switzerland. The front is gold cloisonné work inlaid with garnets and mounted with gems, and in the centre, a contemporary glass paste.

117 Front panel of an eighth-century reliquary casket decorated with pierced bone panels, showing the figure of Christ in the centre and on the left, and an angel on the right. The plaques that decorate this casket are no longer in the original positions for which they were designed.

pierced and carved bone plaques preserved in the church at Werden, near Essen, although not as closely linked with manuscript art as the Fleury reliquary, and much altered in the composition of its decorative panels, again shows the growing importance of a Christian art. Figures in the position of 'Orans' with their arms raised in prayer as on the sarcophagus of Agilbert, interlace and geometric ornament all emphasize this.

Chapter Six

Prelude to Empire

In the early eighth century the pace of the development of a Christian culture in western Europe gathered speed and grew in significance. St Willibrord, born in Northumbria in 658, had begun his missionary work in eastern lands of Friesland in about 690. In 695 he established the bishopric of Wiltaburg, later to be known as Utrecht, and two years later he founded the monastery of Echternach under the patronage of Plectrude, wife of Pepin of Heristal. So far, the indigenous traditions and stylistic links with the eastern Mediterranean have been emphasized in the art of Frankish monasteries. It would, however, be wrong to underestimate the strong and growing influence of Insular art. Indeed, it would be surprising if the widespread missionary activities of British ecclesiastics were to have had no effect on Frankish art.

Such a major manuscript as the Echternach Gospels (Paris, 118 Bibl. Nat. MS. Lat. 9389), written and illuminated at the end of the seventh century for Willibrord's new foundation, either in Northumbria, or by a Northumbrian monk at Echternach itself, proves the close contact with Anglo-Saxon art. In a less obvious way, the Merovingian manuscripts discussed earlier provide evidence of such Insular influence. It is true that much of the ornamental vocabulary and the loose, less rigid and less 'metallic' techniques of these manuscripts set them apart from contemporary Anglo-Saxon work, but here and there, quite intricate interlace, precise key patterns and interlaced animal forms indicate some knowledge of Insular styles. But above all, the organization of the whole page, as for example the opening folios of the Sacramentaries of Gellone and Gelasius, shows that the emphasis on the opening of the sacred text, with a large first initial and

118   A page from the Echternach Gospels, showing the evangelist symbol of St Matthew. A superb late-seventh-century manuscript, closely related to the Lindisfarne Gospels in the British Museum, and an early export of Insular art to the Continent, perhaps already during Willibrord's mission.

119   The opening page of the text of the Lindisfarne Gospels (Brit. Mus. Cotton MS. Nero. D. IV. fol. 3), written at the monastery of Lindisfarne, off the coast of Northumbria, *c*. 700. It shows one of the finest examples of the decorative treatment of a page of text of a kind developed in England, which was to have considerable influence in the Frankish kingdom (*see for example Illus. 100*)

letters arranged in blocks across the page slowly diminishing in size, is exactly parallel to contemporary Insular practice, both in the Northumbrian and the Canterbury schools of illumination. This is likely to mean that local painters, using their own techniques and well-established ornamental forms have followed the lay-out of imported books. In metalwork, also, some high-quality imports survive. The small silver house-shrine preserved at Mortain (Manche), bearing a runic inscription and busts of Christ between SS. Michael and Gabriel, is one such piece, and the large and magnificent processional cross preserved at Bischofshofen parish church, near Salzburg, is another. It is a wooden cross, covered in bronze-gilt, embossed with intricate Insular interlace mounted along its edges and inhabited foliate scrolls on its front and back. A small number of glass-pastes, some decorated with spiral ornaments, survive on it, and take the place of the more usual mounted gems. A twelfth-century tradition records that it is the gift of St Rupertus, who was Bishop of Salzburg at the beginning of the eighth century. It is undoubtedly the work of a goldsmith trained in England, the style of the inhabited scrolls being very close to the mid-eighth-century Ormside bowl preserved in the York Museum.

119

120, 121

The greatest of the Anglo-Saxon missionaries and the 'Apostle of the Germans' was Wynfrith, born about 675 at Kirton in Devonshire. When he travelled to the Continent his first call was not on the Frankish Court, or the Rhemish archbishops, but on Rome. He undertook the conversion of the German tribes by Papal authority under his new Roman name of Boniface. He began his work with Willibrord in Friesland between 716 and 721, and was active after that in central Germany. In 722 he was created Bishop by Gregory II and in 732 received the pallium as Archbishop from Pope Gregory III. During these years Charles Martel, the ruling Mayor of the Palace, seems to have taken little interest in Boniface's activities, but when Charles died in 741, and the power

120, 121 Anglo-Saxon wooden processional cross, covered in embossed gilt-bronze, preserved in the parish church of Bischofshofen near Salzburg. The glass pastes with spiral decoration are examples of the very late survival of indigenous Celtic patterns. The very high-quality inhabited scroll ornament can only be paralleled in the work of Insular goldsmiths of the eighth century

was divided between his two sons Pepin and Carloman, the latter, who received the office of Mayor and the eastern half of the kingdom, summoned the recently created Archbishop. From now on began a new era of co-operation between Church and State, which was to set the pattern for centuries to come. Boniface was commissioned to reform the entire Frankish Church, and Carloman undertook to enforce the decrees of the synods of bishops by incorporating them as carpitularies in the law. The holders of high ecclesiastic office became great lords, were given great financial resources in land and enjoyed military support, which enabled them to pursue the conversion of pagan tribes by force, rather than by peaceful mission. St Boniface himself founded four new bishoprics east of the Rhine, at Fritzlar (741), Erfurt (741), Würzburg (741) and Eichstätt (745) and re-organized five more. He also created what he called a 'model' monastery at Fulda in 744, governed by the rules of St Benedict. In 755, at Dokkum in Friesland, he suffered martyrdom.

In return for the generous support of the Church by the State, the secular power enjoyed the loyalty of the prelates and, on the whole, virtually controlled the appointment to high ecclesiastic office, especially to bishoprics. Carloman's brother Pepin also carried out reforms in Neustria, and with the same aim of strengthening the central secular authority. When Carloman resigned his office in 747 and withdrew to the monastery of Monte Cassino, where he died in 754, Pepin the Short became sole ruler and in 751, as mentioned earlier, was anointed King of the Franks, in name and in fact.

The coronation of Pepin, with the Pope's blessing, marks the break with the Merovingian age and the beginning of the Carolingian, and in a sense, his coronation and the title of *Patricius Romanus*, which used to be assumed by the Exarch of Ravenna who was the representative of the Emperor in Italy, bestowed on Pepin by Pope Stephen II two years later, foreshadowed the imperial coronation of Charlemagne in the year 800.

But more than mere symbolism connects the achievements of Pepin the Short with those of his great son Charles. In his relatively short reign, from 751 until 768, he laid the foundations for most of the policies on which Charlemagne was to build. They included the greater centralization and royal control over economic and monetary policy, the extension of Frankish royal power over the often recalcitrant nobles, especially on the borders of the kingdom, and the creation of a new relationship with the Papacy based on mutual advantage.

The expansion of monastic landed wealth continued under the Carolingians, but under Pepin the Short, and even more so under Charlemagne, there was also to be an expansion of public control over the economy and a serious attempt at the planning of it. Pepin and his advisers began by attacking the problem at its roots, the reform and purification of money. The earliest known cartulary was issued by Pepin in July 755. It decreed that there shall henceforth be no more than 22 solidi in one livre, that the moneyer was allowed to take one and the remainder shall be handed over to their rightful owner. It is clear that the King had begun to attempt to exercise central control over the minting of money. Some thirty years later, Charlemagne imposed a new standard, a division of the livre into 20 solidi and of the solidus into 12 deniers, and the striking of silver coins worth one denier for wide and general circulation. This division, which was continued for many centuries, survived in Britain until our own day. But even Charlemagne never fully realised his aim of a royal monopoly for the minting of currency.

But a sound monometallic currency was established, and the cartularies issued show how much more the early Carolingians were concerned about the problems of economics as a source for the strength of central government, than their Merovingian predecessors. Above all, they were concerned to create a monetary system that was realistic and answered people's fundamental needs. Not the demands of large scale international commerce were uppermost in their minds, but internal trade, and even local markets. Small silver deniers and half-deniers served to enable people to buy a pound of bread or a gallon of wine.

A similar desire for the centralization of power underlies Pepin's relationships with the nobles within, and on the borders of, his kingdom. In eight campaigns in eight years, from 752 to 759, he subdued Aquitaine, partly by force of arms, partly by negotiation and even by the murder of the Duke of Aquitaine. At the same time he extended his control in the south to include Septimania, the old Visigothic area on the Mediterranean coast.

By far the most important and the most significant of Pepin's policies for the later history of Europe, was the extension of Frankish interests in Italy. In January of 754, Pope Stephen II arrived at Pepin's villa of Ponthion on the Marne to ask for the help of the Franks against his neighbours, the Lombards. In 751 the Lombards had conquered the Exarchy of Ravenna, and the threat to the temporal power of the Pope had grown until King Aistulf was threatening the Roman *ducatus* itself. An alliance was formed, and Pepin undertook to assist and protect the Papacy, and to restore to the Pope the Exarchy as well as the *Respublica Romanorum* conquered by Aistulf. Pepin crossed the Alps and in two campaigns defeated the King, restored the temporal power of the Pope in Rome and granted the Papacy the provinces of Central Italy, which had been the property of the Byzantine Emperor. It marked the final break of the ancient alliance of the Chair of St Peter with the legitimate Roman Emperor in Constantinople, which had ceased to be of any real importance since the outbreak of the iconoclastic controversy in the second quarter of the century.

It was probably at this time that the famous 'Donation of Constantine' to Pope Silvester I was forged. The donation survives only in a ninth-century copy. Its object was to give authority to Pope Stephen, who had, as incumbent of the

Chair of St Peter, been granted temporal sovereignty over Italy and the west by the first Christian Emperor, and to confer on Pepin the title of Patrician, and later, for the Pope to confer on Pepin's son, Charlemagne, the title of Emperor, and to consecrate him.

If Pepin the Short, when he died in 768, left other problems – Brittany, Saxony and Bavaria, for example – for his sons to face, it is true to say that the policy which Charlemagne was so triumphantly to carry out, was conceived by Pepin. And yet, his reign was only a 'prelude to Empire'. His work was to be overshadowed by Charlemagne's Western Empire, with a 'Second Rome' as the Court poets were to call it, created at Aachen. If no real break of continuity can be seen in the political, economic and administrative fields between what was initiated by Pepin and achieved by Charlemagne, there can be no doubt that it was the Emperor crowned in Rome thirty-two years after his father's death who inspired a cultural revival in north-western Europe which was to give direction to European civilization for centuries to come. In the end, only the foundations had been laid on which Charlemagne was to build his Carolingian 'Renovatio'.

Bibliography

ÅBERG, N., *Die Franken und Westgoten in der Völkerwanderungszeit.* Uppsala, 1922.

—, *The Occident and the Orient in the Art of the Seventh Century, The Merovingian Empire.* Stockholm, 1947.

BAUM, J., *La sculpture figurale en Europe à l'époque Mérovingienne.* Paris, 1937.

BEHRENS, G., *Merovingerzeit.* Mainz, 1947.

BURY, J. BAGNELL, *The Invasion of Europe by the Barbarians, A Series of Lectures.* London, 1928.

CHRIST, Y., *Les Cryptes Mérovingiennes de l'Abbaye de Jouarre.* Paris, 1955.

DOPPELFELD, O., 'Das fränkische Frauengrab unter dem Chor des Kölner Domes', in *Germania,* Vol. 38 (1960).

DOPSCH, A., *The Economic and Social Foundations of European Civilization.* New York, 1937.

ELBERN, V. H., *Das Erste Jahrtausend.* Düsseldorf, 1962.

GRABAR, A. and NORDENFALK, C., *Early Medieval Painting.* Lausanne, 1957.

GREGORY OF TOURS, *The History of the Franks* (trs. by O. M. Dalton). 2 vols. London, 1927.

HACKENBROCH, Y., *Italienisches Email des frühen Mittelalters.* Basel, 1938.

HAWKES, S. C., 'Soldiers and Settlers in Britain', in *Medieval Archaeology,* Vol. 5 (1961).

HOLMQUIST, W., *Kunstprobleme der Merovingerzeit.* Stockholm, 1939.

—, *Germanic Art during the first Millennium A.D.* Stockholm, 1955.

HUBERT, J., *L'Art pré-roman.* Paris, 1938.

HUBERT, J., PORCHER, J. and VOLBACH, W. F., *Europe in the Dark Ages.* London, 1969.

JENNY, W. A. VON, *Die Kunst der Germanen im Frühen Mittelalter.* Berlin, 1940.

LAISTNER, M. L. W., *Thought and Letters in Western Europe, A.D. 500 to 900.* London, 1931.

LATOUCHE, R., *The Birth of Western Economy.* London, 1961.

LOT, F., *The End of the Ancient World and the Beginning of the Middle Ages.* New York, 1931.

MOSS, H. ST. L. B., *The Birth of the Middle Ages, 394–814.* 2nd ed. London, 1947.

PIRENNE, H., *Mohammed and Charlemagne.* London, 1939.

RADEMACHER, F., *Fränkische Goldscheibenfibeln aus dem Rheinischen Landesmuseum in Bonn.* Munich, 1940.

SALIN, B., *Die altgermanische Thierornamentik.* Stockholm, 1904.

SALIN, E., *La civilisation Mérovingienne* (ed. by A. and J. Picard & Cie), 4 vols. Paris, 1949–59.

—, 'Les tombes gallo-romaines et mérovingiennes de la basilique de Saint-Denis', in *Acad. des inscriptions et belles-lettres,* XLIV, 1, 1960.

131

TSCHUMI, O., *Burgunder, Alamannen und Langobarden in der Schweiz*. Berne, 1945.

VEECK, W., *Die Alamannen in Württemberg*. 2 vols. Berlin and Leipzig, 1931.

WALLACE-HADRILL, J. M., *The Long-haired Kings and other Studies in Frankish History*. London, 1962.

—, *The Barbarian West, 400–1000*. London, 1952.

WILSON, D. M., *The Anglo-Saxons*. London, 1960.

ZIMMERMAN, E. H., *Vorkarolingische Miniaturen*. 4 vols. Berlin, 1916.

CATALOGUES OF EXHIBITIONS

L'art mérovingien, Musées Royaux d'Art et d'Histoire. Brussels, 1954.

Werdendes Abendland an Rhein und Ruhr. Essen, 1956.

List of Illustrations

The author and publishers are grateful to the many official bodies, institutions and individuals mentioned below for their assistance in supplying original illustration material. Illustrations without acknowledgment are from originals in Thames & Hudson's archives.

St Jean. Photo Archives
Photographiques.

27, 28 Capital and column from
Notre-Dame de la Dourade,
Toulouse. Musée des Augustins,
Toulouse, and Louvre, Paris.

29 Genealogy of the Merovingian
monarchs, 481–751. Drawn by
John Woodcock.

30 Grave-goods from a Frankish
cemetery at Herpes, Charente.
British Museum. Photo John
Webb.

31 Group of Frankish grave-goods
from northern France and the
Rhineland. British Museum. Photo
John Webb.

32 Gold coin of Theodobert,
533–48. British Museum. Photo
Ray Gardner.

33 S-shaped brooches from
Diesslingen. Landesmuseum,
Stuttgart. Museum photo.

34 Fish-shaped brooches from
Bülach. Swiss National Museum,
Zurich. Museum photo.

35 Gold and garnet brooch from
Wittislingen. Bayerisches
Nationalmuseum, Munich. Photo
Max Hirmer.

36 Silver-gilt fibula from
Wittislingen. Bayerisches
Nationalmuseum, Munich. Photo
Max Hirmer.

37 Helmet from a warrior's grave at
Morken. Rheinisches Landesmuseum,
Bonn, Museum photo.

38–40 Glass beaker, shield-boss and
bronze bowl from a warrior's grave
at Morken. Rheinisches
Landesmuseum, Bonn. Museum
photo.

41–43 Grave-goods from the burial
of a Frankish princess below Cologne
Cathedral. Römisch Germanisches
Museum, Cologne. Photos courtesy
of Professor Dr O. Doppelfeld.

44, 45 Glass vessels and helmet from
the burial of a six-year-old boy below
Cologne Cathedral. Römisch
Germanisches Museum, Cologne.
Photos courtesy of Professor
Dr O. Doppelfeld.

46–48 Pin and brooches from the
coffin of Queen Arnegunde, St Denis,
Paris. Trésor de la Basilique,
St Denis. Photos Archives
Photographiques.

49, 50 Reconstruction drawing and
plan of the coffin of Queen
Arnegunde.

51, 52 Buckles, strap-ends and ring
of Queen Arnegunde. Trésor de la
Basilique, St Denis.

53 Silver-gilt bracteate from
Gotland. Photo ATA, Stockholm.

54 Gold coin of Dagobert, 629–39.
British Museum. Photo Ray
Gardner.

55 Gold coin of Charibert II, d. 630.
British Museum. Photo Ray
Gardner.

56 Family tree of the Mayors of the
Palace and ancestors of Charlemagne.
Drawn by John Woodcock.

57 Map: the spread of monasteries in Europe. Drawn by A. Wilbur after Prinz.

58 Reliquary of St Croix, Poitiers, from an eighteenth-century drawing.

59, 60 Wooden reading desk of St Radegund. Couvent des Dames de Saint-Croix, Poitiers.

61 Frankish belt-buckle from Amiens, Somme. British Museum. Photo John Webb.

62 Coptic tapestry with interlace. Whitworth Art Gallery, Manchester. Photo Elsam, Mann & Cooper.

63 Coptic bronze bowl from near Mainz. British Museum. Photo John Webb.

64 Tombstone of Bishop Boethius from Carpentras. Chapelle Notre-Dame de Vic. Photo John Webb.

65 Bronze altar cross. Kunsthistorisches Museum, Vienna. Museum photo.

66 Panel from choir screen from St Pierre aux Nonnais. Musée de Metz. Museum photo.

67 Grave stele of Rhodia from Kom Buljeh, Fayum. Staatliche Museen zu Berlin, D.D.R. Museum photo.

68 Early Christian sarcophagus from Gaul. Musée de Toulouse. Photo Archives Photographiques.

69 Coptic tapestry with hunting saint from Akhmin. British Museum. Photo Peter Clayton.

70 Funerary stele of a horseman from Hornhausen. Landesmuseum für Vorgeschichte, Halle. Museum photo.

71 Gold disc-brooch from Pliezhausen. Württembergisches Landesmuseum, Stuttgart. Drawn by I. Mackenzie-Kerr.

72 Openwork disc from Oberesslingen. Stadtmuseum, Esslingen.

73 Ornamental shield-plaque from San Pietro, Stabio. Historisches Museum, Berne.

74 Bronze Frankish ornament. British Museum. Photo John Webb.

75 Detail from the so-called sarcophagus of St Calentius. Musée de Bourges. Photo Giraudon.

76 Burgundian belt-buckle. Musée d'Art et d'Histoire, Fribourg. Museum photo.

77 Burgundian bronze belt-buckle. Musée Archéologique, Dijon. Museum photo.

78 Ivory buckle of St Caesarius from the church of Saint-Trophine, Notre-Dame-la-Major, Arles. Photo Archives Photographiques.

79 Pottery St Menas flask. British Museum. Photo Peter Clayton.

80 Ivory pyx with St Menas. British Museum. Photo Max Hirmer.

81 Carved panel from Gondorf. Rheinisches Landesmuseum, Bonn. Museum photo.

82, 83 Frankish tombstone from Niederdollendorf. Rheinisches Landesmuseum, Bonn. Museum photos.

84 Stele from Moselkern. Rheinisches Landesmuseum, Bonn. Museum photo.

85 Gold and garnet brooch from Minden, near Trier. Rheinisches Landesmuseum, Trier. Photo Stadbildstelle, Aachen.

86 Gold disc-brooch from Kärlich. Rheinisches Landesmuseum, Bonn. Drawn by Tony Birks.

87 Gold brooch from Castel Trosino. Museo Nazionale, Rome. Photo GFN.

88 Gold brooch with cameo from Mölsheim. Hessisches Landesmuseum, Darmstadt. Museum photo.

89 The chalice of Chelles. Photo Courtauld Institute of Art.

90 Bewcastle Cross. Photo National Monuments Record.

91 Ruthwell Cross. Photo National Monuments Record.

92 Crypt of St Ebrigisile, Jouarre. Photo Giraudon.

93 West wall, crypt of St Paul, Abbaye de Notre Dame, Jouarre.

94 Crypt of St Paul, Abbaye de Notre Dame, Jouarre.

95 Marble capitals, crypt of St Paul, Abbaye de Notre Dame, Jouarre. Photo Archives Photographiques.

96 Sarcophagus of Abbess Theodochilde. Abbaye de Notre Dame, Jouarre. Photo Archives Photographiques.

97 Sarcophagus of Bishop Agilbert. Abbaye de Notre Dame, Jouarre. Photo Archives Photographiques.

98 Head of the sarcophagus of Bishop Agilbert. Photo courtesy Dr G. Zarnecki.

99 Apse of Hosios David, Salonica. Photo Max Hirmer.

100–102 Illuminations from the Sacramentary of Gelasius. Biblioteca Apostolica Vaticana (Reg. Lat. 316). Museum photos.

103, 104 Decorated pages from the Gellone Sacramentary. Bibliothèque Nationale, Paris (Lat. 12048). Museum photos.

105 Illumination from the Chronicle of Fredegar. Bibliothèque Nationale, Paris (Lat. 10910). Museum photo.

106 Cividale, Ratchis altar. Photo Brisighelli.

107, 108 Miniature paintings from the Gospel Book of Gundohinus. Bibliothèque Municipale, Autun (MS. lat. 3).

109, 110 Ornamental manuscript illuminations from the Commentary of St Jerome. Bibliothèque Nationale, Paris (lat. 11627), and the *History of the World* by Orosius, Laon, Bibl. Municipal (MS. 137).

111 Porta della Pescheria, Modena Cathedral. Photo Orlandini.

112 Ornamental manuscript illumination from the Laon MS. Bibliothèque Nationale, Paris (lat. 12168). Museum photo.

113 The Warnebertus reliquary. Stiftsbibliothek, Beromünster. Museum photo.

114 St Mummole reliquary. Abbey church of Fleury. Photo Archives Photographiques.

115 Reliquary from Nymegen. Aartsbisschoppelijke Musea, Utrecht. Museum photo.

116 St Maurice d'Agaune reliquary. Abbaye de St Maurice. Photo Benedikt Rast.

117 Detail of the casket of St Liudger. Abbey church of Werden. Photo Marburg.

118 Page with St Mathew symbol, Echternach Gospels. Bibliothèque Nationale (Lat. 9389. fol. 18 v).

119 Opening page of Lindisfarne Gospels. British Museum (Cotton MS. Nero D. IV. fol. 3).

120, 121 Processional cross of Rupertus. Parish church of Bischofshofen.

Index

Numbers in *italics* refer to illustrations